"Dana Wood has masterfully blended humor with hugely helpful information for any mama who wants to re-boot her life—mind, body, and soul! Her tips and stories are simple, but transformational. And by the end of the book, you feel like you have a new friend who is just a few steps ahead, shining the light to make your path easier and more delightful."

—**Kathy Freston**, author of *Quantum Wellness:*
A Practical and Spiritual Guide to Health and Happiness

"*Momover* reads like a juicy exposé that spills a delicious secret: a happy mom equals a happy baby. Dana Wood redefines the tenets of modern motherhood with wit and a stockpile of indispensable, expert advice."

—**Cynthia Rowley**

"Hip, insightful, funny, and filled with practical wisdom, *Momover* is packed with helpful, hardcore information on the pitfalls of mothering—warts and all—and reads like you are talking with your best friend. Using her years of expertise in the beauty world, her whip-smart mind, and *mucho* common sense, Dana Wood takes you from the brink of disaster after giving birth to the wondrous discovery of an even better version of the old you! I urge you to share her journey. Not only will you laugh along the way, but by following her wisdom, you will be transformed."

—**Dayle Haddon**, actress, model, and author of *Ageless Beauty: A*
Woman's Guide to Lifelong Beauty and Well-Being

"After you have a baby, everyone focuses on the baby and the baby clothing and baby gear. I applaud Dana Wood for turning her attention to the new mother and helping her return to her chic fabulous self!"

—**Liz Lange**, founder and president of
Liz Lange Maternity Clothing

mom·over

The New Mom's Guide to
GETTING IT BACK TOGETHER
(even if you never had it in the first place!)

Dana Wood
Foreword by Veronica Webb

adamsmedia
Avon, Massachusetts

Published by Adams Media,
a division of F+W Media, Inc.
57 Littlefield Street, Avon, MA 02322. U.S.A.
www.adamsmedia.com

ISBN 10: 1-4405-0030-4
ISBN 13: 978-1-4405-0030-5

Printed in the United States of America.

10 9 8 7 6 5 4 3 2 1

Library of Congress Cataloging-in-Publication Data
is available from the publisher.

This publication is designed to provide accurate and authoritative information with regard
to the subject matter covered. It is sold with the understanding that the publisher is not
engaged in rendering legal, accounting, or other professional advice. If legal advice or
other expert assistance is required, the services of a competent professional person should
be sought.

—From a *Declaration of Principles* jointly adopted by a Committee of the
American Bar Association and a Committee of Publishers and Associations

Many of the designations used by manufacturers and sellers to distinguish their products are claimed as trademarks. Where those designations appear in this book and Adams
Media was aware of a trademark claim, the designations have been printed with initial
capital letters.

The information and advice provided in this book are meant to serve as a resource, and
should not be used as a substitute for the specific guidance of your own physicians. For any
concerns of a physical, mental, or emotional nature, always seek the expert opinion of your
doctors and other trusted caregivers.

This book is available at quantity discounts for bulk purchases.
For information, call 1-800-289-0963.

acknowledgments

to my mamas:

Christine, Elizabeth, Gwen, Jeanine, Jenny B., Jenny R., Jill E., Jill S., Katherine, Mara, Melissa, Ninka, Patricia, and Rebekah.

Thank you for sharing your heartwarming and hilarious tales from the trenches.

to my experts:

Christina Attiken; Jill Baron, MD; Michele Bernhardt; Erika Bloom; Fredric Brandt, MD; La Reine Chabut; Helen Garabedian; Anthony Gianzero; Sonia Kashuk; Michael Kane, MD; Alexander Kulick, MD; Jackie Keller; David Kirsch; Gregg Lituchy, DDS; Tanya Mackay; Jeffrey Morrison, MD; Sari Nisker; Lucy Puryear, PhD; Casey Soer; Bria Simpson; Lyss Stern; Julie Tupler, RN; Alycea Ungaro; and Vanessa Wauchope.

Thank you for making time to provide guidance and help to so many new mamas.

to "the pilars":

Guzman and Queen

Thank you for providing the bully pulpit and push I needed to make this book happen.

to "stine":

Thank you for helping me carve out time to write and for making our lives work so seamlessly.

to hubby:

Thank you for your love, support, and countless 3:00 A.M. pep talks.

to my beloved diapered darling:

Thank you for turning my life on its head in the absolutely, positively best way possible.

table of contents

foreword

There was never a doubt in my mind that I'd have kids. Of course I did focus on a few other things prior to setting my sights on motherhood and I waited until I was good and ready—physically, emotionally, and spiritually—and had a million adventures under my belt before I took the plunge. But I always knew that "Mom" would be a big part of my ultimate job description, the role of a lifetime that I was destined to play.

Yet even with all that "prep" work, I still wasn't truly primed for the tidal wave of personal change a woman goes through after giving birth. For me, postpartum was the most profoundly elating and devastating feeling I've ever had (twice) in my life. At first, my focus turned totally away from the outside world and my inner life and I put everything I had toward the welfare of my two little beings. That sounds reasonable, right? Isn't that what moms are supposed to do? But today when I see other new mothers who are in the same self-righteous state of self-deprivation as I was, I realize that I wouldn't even hire someone in that state to babysit, let alone look to them as a healthy example of motherhood.

Physically recovering from childbirth was also challenging. I had two C-sections in a span of 18 months, with a gall bladder removal on top of that! All this triggered a tremendous loss in muscle tone and strength. I also gained around 60 pounds, which was approximately half of my pre-baby body weight. So I went from being a physically strong person—a diver, a yogi, a runner, and a dancer—to barely being able to pick myself up off the floor.

But happily, my martyr days are firmly behind me. I now make my mental, physical, and spiritual health my number one priority —which is, of course, the core premise of the book you're wisely holding in your hands right now. Obviously caring for my kids is still right up there in terms of importance and it's a constant juggling act to keep everything in balance, but I need to put myself first and exercise, eat well, and communicate clearly in order to feel centered and grounded.

My children are my greatest achievement and my greatest joy, but they're also an endless source of questions and challenges that require constant study, prayer, and patience. And it's hard to be there for them if I'm not there for myself. It took a while for me to find my footing with this whole mom thing, but, from one mama to another, I know you'll get to the right destination on your journey. Just remember that every Momover begins with a single step.

—Veronica Webb

introduction

mom·over

(noun) : MASHUP OF "MOM" AND "MAKEOVER" minus the pressure to look like a total babe 24/7. *(Unless that's what the mama wants, of course.)* Holistic; ENCOMPASSES MIND, BODY, AND SPIRIT. Nudges her to take primo care of herself, with zero guilt & tons of support. BENEFICIAL TO ENTIRE FAMILY.

I remember it as if it were yesterday. There's me, lying on a blankie on a sweet patch of park behind my New York City apartment building. Beautiful day, the sun was shining, and there I was, blubbering like a whale as I rubbed Coppertone into my pudgy belly and spider-veined thighs. I had recently given birth to my first child, a bouncing baby girl. But, while she was crazy-healthy and completely in charge of the world around her, I was a mess. And as the tears streamed down, it dawned on me that there was no way I was going to recoup my formerly sky-high energy level, laser-sharp focus, and once-great ass unless I expended an insane amount of effort and elbow grease.

In short, I needed a Momover—mentally, physically, and spiritually. And the only one who could give it to me, was, well, me. Sure, I'd have to call in a fleet of gurus for guidance and I'd have to pawn the Diapered Darling (DD for short) off on Hubby for a few hours here and there while I went about the business of looking and feeling fab, but the motivation to hop off the new-mommy self-pity train and get with a new and improved postbaby program had to come from moi and moi alone.

At the time of this major life epiphany, I was the health and beauty director of *Cookie*, a short-lived but beloved magazine for stylish moms. In a rare flash of genius, I decided to take advantage of my perch at *Cookie* to embark on a "back-from-the-brink" health and beauty journey, and document it all in an online column. Thus, the cyber version of *Momover* was hatched shortly after I figured out I needed one myself. In the kickoff column, I detailed my master plan. With the help of all the expert sources I've accumulated in my twenty-plus years as a health and beauty journalist, I'd work through a litany of baby-induced bummers—kangaroo pouch, squiggly veins, and fat ass included—and report back to my fellow mama bears if I found any remedies (quick or otherwise) that actually worked. Yes, I wanted to look like a mom-babe, but I also wanted to help other women feel like their own cooing little DDs hadn't completely capsized their lives.

But first, I set a few ground rules: After I tried something, many people needed to notice and comment favorably upon it; any cockamamie procedure I indulged in had to be at least partially grounded in reality, meaning it was something "real moms" would actually do; and as the ultimate litmus test for a spoiled-rotten beauty editor such as myself, it had to be something I'd plunk down my own cold hard cash for.

Granted, I set the bar ridiculously high; my first "wish list" was based on the stellar physical features of some of the sexiest, strongest moms on the planet. I wanted legs like Elle Macpherson's, abs like Heidi Klum's, arms like Uma Thurman's (circa her ripped "Kill Bill" era), and energy like Madonna's. Since then, I've played human guinea pig for all manner of après-baby beautifiers, from electro-shock therapy on my belly and laser tooth whitening to seaweed appetite suppressants and tracking my steps from dawn till dusk with a decidedly unchic clip-on pedometer.

But something happened on the road to Superficiality Central: I started to become a lot more concerned with the way I felt than the way I looked. As an older first-time mom, there was already a long list of beauty woes headed my way. Still, as I progressed along my little self-absorbed journey, I started connecting more and more dots between the inside and the outside and with the very cool way that feeling centered and calm miraculously made me look younger. (Seriously, I'm convinced soaking in a hot bath filled with yummy essential oils immediately erases five years from my face.) Today, my "quest" includes a nice mix of inner and outer beautifiers from deep-breathing exercises to professional eyebrow shaping. But if I'm leaning in any particular direction these days, it's toward wellness much more than surface gloss. In other words, if I'm too tired at bedtime to condition my hair *and* dry brush my skin to boost my immune system, the dry brushing will win every time.

And about those celebrity role models I mentioned earlier: Yes, they're gorgeous. And most of them look like they could leap tall buildings in a single bound. But I don't spend a lot of time wishing I resembled someone else. Rather, I just want to borrow some of their self-discipline because I totally believe in the magical powers of focus, determination, and hard work. And anyone looking at Elle Macpherson or Heidi Klum knows that they do, too.

But truly the best, and really the only, reason to embark on a Momover is because you want to be the best you possible. Don't let anyone guilt-trip you about taking the time you need to achieve that goal. It's your right to continue to primp and take world-class care of yourself—drumroll please—even after the baby arrives. Maybe pre-DD your life was a never-ending circuit of facials, mani/pedis, kick-boxing classes, and Restylane injections. Or perhaps you weren't 1,000 percent invested in the whole perfection trip, but still wanted to look damn good on a daily basis. Wherever you fell on the maintenance scale, the point is you were on it; you were in the game. Now that your tot has arrived (an absolute blessing of course, just not for your thighs), you want to reclaim at least a little of your former self. You want to look better. But equally important, you want to feel better. Bursting with energy; ready to embrace your new life with your DD on your hip and your mascara wand in hand.

So here's the Momover mantra, which I insist you commit to memory right this very nano-second: *Treating yourself well will have a positive trickle-down effect on every aspect of your life, including your relationship with your delicious tot.* Centered, happy mom = centered, happy baby (don't laugh; a calm, peaceful newborn is the holy grail for new mothers). While that's a simple concept to wrap your mind around, it's not always so simple to follow, especially when there are exponentially more demands on you and your time than ever before.

about this book

I'm not a doctor, a personal trainer, a makeup artist, or a life coach. Instead, I'm an insanely curious journalist who just happened to have had a baby late in life and was thrown for a mental, physical, and spiritual loop. Mix those two elements together—dogged reporter meets freaked-out older first-time mom—and you get Momover, the go-to tool I wish I'd had tucked away in my hospital bag when I delivered.

By fixating on my outer postdelivery self when I really needed to be getting my head straight as a clueless "first-timer," I probably didn't tackle my own Momover in the most optimal way. That's why I've laid it all out for you here in a mind, body, and spirit format. In Part 1: Getting It Together Mentally, you'll focus on making that often maddeningly tough transition to life with Baby; the best way to ride the postpartum hormone rollercoaster; and building new networks of helpers, infant experts, and fellow moms. Part 2: Getting It Together Physically, is all about the nitty-gritty body stuff, including recovering lost nutrients and energy; reining in a jiggly midsection; and the pros and cons of attempting a DIY microdermabrasion or bang trim. The final section, Part 3: Getting It Together Emotionally and Spiritually, is a just crunchy-enough plan of action for training yourself to be mindful of your internal dialogue; strategies for defusing stress; and tips for achieving a good night's sleep. (Pinkie swear: It's doable.)

Of course, all of those "parts" are interconnected—that's the holistic approach that I both strive for myself and, after having done so much research, the one I also feel is the most beneficial for all new mothers. Consequently, you'll see certain subthemes repeated throughout the book. For instance, I'm a big believer in actively corralling and harnessing your thoughts and really focusing, so you'll see that notion woven through several chapters. And while no one is saying that you can't flip straight to the section on saggy boobs ("Breast Intentions," Chapter 11) in Part 2, you might want to read at least a snippet of the first few chapters before diving in to "fix" whatever you're convinced needs fixing.

After reading a bit of Part 3, you might just decide, all Zen like, that you're fine just the way you are. It's your Momover, after all.

Finally, here's the 411 on all the extras you'll find in every chapter and the monster resource appendix at the end of the book.

- **Worked for Me:** Consider these my own personal bag of tricks, gleaned through a combination of trial and error and interviews with experts. While some went the way of the bottle warmers and Baby Einstein DVDs, I've incorporated lots of the other lifestyle changes I made postdelivery—such as ditching Diet Coke and balancing my pH level—into my life permanently.

- **Reserve the Right to . . . :** Mostly, these tip boxes are little "escape clauses" to deploy when all the babying gets to be too much (such as zapping the guilt and hanging a "Do Not Disturb" sign on the bedroom door when relatives are in town). But I also get serious at times, as when I recommend peppering your doctors with questions and demanding access to your medical records.

- **Mother Load:** Often hilarious, at times painful, these are the stories I've gathered from fellow mothers far and wide. You'll meet my "mom squad" as the chapters unfold, but to protect the innocent, they're identified only by their first names. As a sneak peek, here are the mamas who will be telling their tales: Christine, Elizabeth, Gwen, Jeanine, Jenny B., Jenny R., Jill E., Jill S., Katherine, Mara, Melissa, Ninka, Patricia, and Rebekah. Is it just me, or do we all feel a little bit more bonded to each other when we spill the dirty diapers on our own lives?

- **Dig Deeper Appendix:** I once read that Scorpios are considered the "detectives of the zodiac." Whether that's true is anyone's guess, but I will say that this particular Scorp is an absolute information freak. But I also believe in cutting to the chase when the situation warrants, so "Dig Deeper" is just a quick download of the books, DVDs, websites, and other resources I've found especially helpful. It's arranged according to chapter, so you can just flip to the back of the book and find more to explore that pertains to what you've just read. Easy-peasy—just what a busy mama needs.

Go for it. And know that I'm with you, every step of the way.

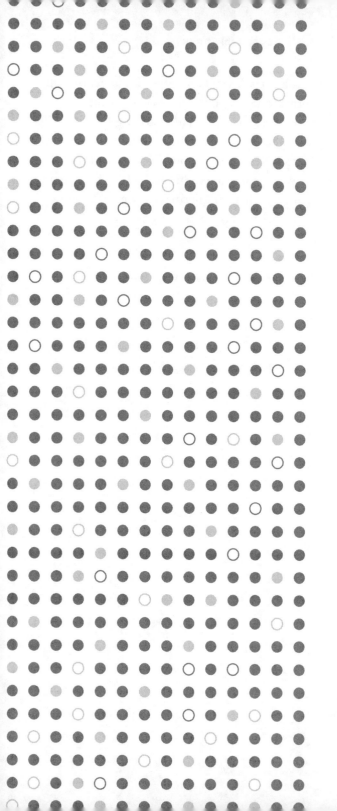

getting it together
mentally

Though it may seem beyond reach in those first few postpartum days, a clear head and a low-key, completely doable strategy for handling hormonal upset can make the transition to new mommyhood much, much easier. In Part 1, you'll get an easy-to-grasp synopsis of what's going on with your body and how that relates to your undoubtedly ultrasensitive postpartum mental and emotional state. You'll also learn how to accept the help that's offered to you (for many women, that's easier said than done), reconnect with friends after the "cocoon" phase, and adjust to your "plus-Baby" identity.

handling home-from-the-hospital freakouts

You spend forty long weeks gearing up for delivery day. You have books piled from here to the ceiling, all dog-eared on the gory bits about what unfolds in the labor ward. Your closet is stocked with plenty of hopefully cute and comfy—albeit tent-like—ensembles. Almost certainly, an extensive birth-prep class is part of the equation, as you and the other mommies-to-be anticipate the momentous occasion in all your waddly, preggo glory. In short, every ounce of mental energy is directed toward Just Getting Through It. "It," of course, being the arrival of your very own Diapered Darling (DD for short) into the open arms of Mama, Papa, and the assorted millions who've gathered to take part in the blessed event.

I'm not mocking. Delivering a baby is a huge deal. I've done it recently enough to know that (and I didn't even have an easy go of it, laborwise, as you'll learn in a bit). But for first timers like me, especially those of us who've had next to no previous interaction with a real/live/breathing/eating/crying/peeing/pooping newborn, bringing that tiny bundle of joy home from the maternity ward is when the real panic sets in.

So here's my advice to those of you who are reading this either before delivery day or shortly thereafter: Feel free to stay in Just Get Through It mode. There's no "wrong" way to do the newborn thing, but there is a painful way to do it, and that's to second-guess yourself all the way through. That tends to lead to a kind of psychological ground zero and before long, you're wondering why you ever decided to have a baby in the first place.

It's my job, in writing this book, to steer you away from all of that useless, energy-draining, second-guessing hooey and point you in a way healthier, much more fun direction. So come along for a soul-searching, no-stones-unturned ride to the magical land of I'm So on Top of My Mama Game.

waaaah!

Though I hate to kick off this happy, peppy book with a tale of woe, I think I have to. Because, in doing so, I'm hoping that I can illustrate that you can live through an edgy, nail-bitten pregnancy, a very dodgy delivery, a postpartum period in which you feel like something that the cat dragged in, and still wind up pinching yourself on a regular basis because you love your baby so insanely much.

So here's my really-not-great story: Conceiving at the age of forty-two after two rounds of IUI (intrauterine insemination, aka "the turkey baster" method of family planning), I sailed through my pregnancy easily—at least physically. Mentally, well, let's just say I've experienced more carefree periods in my life. My long-dormant anxiety flared, and there were even a few nights when I woke Hubby out of a dead sleep, insisting that he take me to the emergency room because I was convinced I was dying of a panic attack. (He didn't take me; I didn't die.)

(Author's Note: Although I refer to my "Hubby" a lot throughout this book, that's only because I happen to have one. Rest assured that I realize that there are plenty of single mama bears out there, as well as lots of other types of nonhubby family scenarios.)

Compounding my anxiety problem was the dastardly condition *cyberchondria*. I'm sure a lot of you have that, too. You know, your eyes suddenly pop open in the middle of the night, you're hyperalert and fretting about some obscure illness, and you sneak off to the home office, fire up the computer, and begin surfing the Internet for every possible worst-case health scenario imaginable. My own personal pregnancy *bête noire* was tied to the advanced age at which I was having my DD. I'd sit there for long stretches of time Googling "amniocentesis results" and "Down syndrome statistics." I know, I know—incredibly unhealthy! But, as I've since learned through speaking to several doctors while researching stories, pregnancy anxiety is extremely common, especially if you have a history of anxiety, which I do, albeit at a mild level. Knowing that pregnancy can retrigger mental anguish helps me cut myself major slack when I think back on those predelivery months and wish that I'd been the laid-back, baby booty-knitting type. And if you were a little panicky while preggo, I urge you to cut yourself some slack, too.

When the Big Day Came

My oh-so-fun pregnancy was followed by a fairly traumatic labor and delivery. Because my DD was late (I guess she really liked it in there), I had to be induced. Still, she wouldn't join us. So after eighteen hours of fruitless labor, my beloved ob-gyn opted for a C-section, which is a perfectly normal scenario and one that we'd discussed at length in the months leading up to my delivery day. And truth be told, I was more than happy to finally get my baby out and into my arms. Although I'd attended an extremely crunchy labor-prep class, one in which "medical intervention" was positioned as the handiwork of the Devil, I tossed all that useless guilt out the hospital window and placed my trust in my doctor.

It's what happened three days after the C-section that hit me like a ton of bricks: a blood transfusion. Nowhere—*anywhere*—on the checklist of Horrible Things That Can Happen When You Have a Baby did I see "Get Really Scary Blood Transfusion." Evidently, I'd lost a lot of blood post C-section, so much so that my health was compromised. (Technically, it's called a postpartum hemorrhage, and it's extremely rare.) As my ob-gyn, who made a special trip into the hospital on a blizzardy Saturday morning just to convince me of the severity of my situation, pointed out, the miniscule risk I was taking in accepting donor blood was far outweighed by the upside: feeling human again. My recovery from labor and the cesarean would take much, much longer if I declined the transfusion. Again, I chose to listen to my doctor. And by the next day, I was beginning to see a teensy-weensy light at the end of a long, dark tunnel.

surrender, supermama

In a perfect universe (one I obviously don't happen to inhabit), everything on Planet Make a Baby would go according to plan. An easy pregnancy would segue seamlessly into a hassle-free postpartum period in which Mom and her DD bond like nobody's business while Hubby smiles cheerfully through an endless round of Huggies runs.

Well, wake up and smell the coffee—decaf if you're breastfeeding. Life almost never unfolds that way. And the sooner you mentally cede control and just give in to Mother Nature's plan for you and your baby, the easier you'll have it. Of course, I'm talking a good game here; as you'll read in "Worked for Me," I actually needed to be less loosey-goosey after coming home from the hospital rather than more.

But for the most part, trying to slam structure on an unwieldy situation is mentally and psychologically exhausting. And as you now know, bringing a newborn home from the maternity ward is the mother of all unwieldy situations. Especially when your hormones are running amok, as they're all but guaranteed to do in the immediate postpartum period.

To find out exactly why new mothers are subjected to this inner turmoil, I consulted psychiatrist Lucy Puryear, the author of *Understanding Your Moods When You're Expecting,* one of my most pawed-over pregnancy books (details in the Dig Deeper Appendix). In this new mama must read, Dr. Puryear recommends crawling under the covers with your baby and staying there for a sizeable chunk of your postpartum period. A mother of four, Dr. Puryear has a wee bit of experience on this front. And, as an expert on the female mind, she knows exactly what she's talking about.

Clearly, for take-charge types, chillaxing with the baby is easier said than done. But that doesn't mean it's impossible. "For those who are super-driven prepregnancy," says Dr. Puryear, "that may mean making lists in bed to delegate, handling some business on a laptop in bed rather than on the phone, or allotting one or two hours a day to work on tasks and making sure the rest of the day is for mom and baby."

No matter what type of new mom you are, those first few weeks are the ideal time to start flexing your "Mom Matters" muscles. By getting in the habit of putting yourself at least somewhere near the top of your priority list now rather than later, it will be easier to reside there permanently, which is the whole point of this book. And it will also help you step back and give yourself the self-care you need when you've been taken utterly hostage by your hormones.

escape from hormone hell

It's hard to overestimate the role hormones play in driving pregnant and postpartum women temporarily crazy. I'm not kidding; hormones, though necessary for survival, can produce some of the lowest lows you'll ever experience. I can remember one particular postpartum crash that scared the sweatpants off me. Thankfully, it was short lived.

Because they have such a vise grip on our moods, I've found it helpful to have a basic understanding of the types of hormones that are coursing through our bodies both during pregnancy and after delivery. Make sure to talk to your doctor about your expectations.

reserve the right to . . .

. . . hammer out a prebirth "contract" with your hubby, partner, or other family members absolving you of all hormone-induced bad behavior for *at least* six weeks postdelivery. With that in hand, you won't compound the misery with an additional dose of guilt. I recommend printing multiple copies and hanging them above the crib, in the master bedroom, and anywhere else in the house you might just lose it.

The Preggo Scenario

From the moment you conceive, long before you suspect something's up and start peeing on little plastic sticks, the placenta starts to build, aided by the hormone HCG (human chorionic gonadotropin), whose job it is to protect the fetus in the early stages of pregnancy. It also cues the release of yet another hormone—a biggie—progesterone. After about two months, HCG peaks and the role of progesterone releaser falls to the placenta. By this time, the fertilized egg has been implanted in the uterus. And the placenta is also hard at work secreting estrogen, yet another baby-protecting hormone. That's all very well and good for the yet-to-be-born DD; you, however, were no doubt feeling pretty damn crummy as these lovely concoctions ricocheted around your body, and contrary to popular myth, all of that crumminess can outlive the first trimester.

The Postpreggo Scenario

If you were hoping for a postpartum reprieve from hormone-driven angst and anxiety, you may have to wait a few weeks longer. After the baby arrives, a major hormonal correction occurs when the placenta is delivered: your progesterone and estrogen levels plummet. At this point, you'll be feeling like a human pinball machine and may very well experience the same type of short-lived crash in mood that I did. It's perfectly natural, of course, but scary nonetheless. That's why it's so freaking important for you to zap any guilt you might be feeling for not being over the moon with happiness every time you gaze at your newborn. It's not you—it's your hormones! Hormonally, "postpartum is almost always harder for most women" than pregnancy, says Dr. Puryear. "But emotions should stabilize greatly by two weeks. By six weeks, you should feel not *entirely* back to normal, but close to it."

In the meantime, think of how convenient it is to wave the little hormone flag whenever you feel like acting like a big old she-bitch. "I decided to blame anything and everything on hormones and lack of sleep," says Mara, mama of two. "And while it made me feel calmer knowing 'this too shall pass,' I was hoping to find the expiration date on the 'Hormonal Frenzy' box, but I just couldn't."

There's a reason there isn't, as Mara puts it, "an expiration date on the 'Hormonal Frenzy' box." And that's because the specifics of that sweet release aren't written in stone. Every new mother is different and experiences her own unique timetable for returning to the Land of Sane and Happy Living. For me, the big mood dips split town fairly early, but I didn't feel what I call "good good" until I was roughly eighteen months postpartum and started taking targeted nutritional supplements prescribed for me by brain expert Eric Braverman, MD (more on those in Chapter 15).

Thankfully, if you're like most new moms, you won't have to endure full-blown postpartum depression, or PPD; according to the American College of Obstetricians and Gynecologists, only about 10 percent of new moms succumb to PPD. And knowing you'll be feeling like your old self again before too long is the best news to come down the pike since you spied that little plus sign on the EPT stick.

So hats off and hallelujah! To speed up your departure from Hormone Hell, be sure to stock your pantry and fridge with calming, mood-stabilizing foods like the ones below. I'll be discussing the food-mood connection in-depth later in the book, so for now, I'll just give you the Fisher-Price version of how the foods listed below can soothe you: they stabilize your blood sugar. Basically, a blood sugar level that's spiking and crashing in a never-ending loop is a surefire recipe for a case of the crazies.

Here are the foods and snacks I found especially helpful postpartum:

- Avocadoes
- Bananas
- Beans
- Cottage cheese
- Dried fruits
- Pumpkin
- Squash
- Sweet potatoes
- Tofu
- Tomatoes
- Turkey
- Walnuts
- Whole grains (i.e., brown rice, whole-wheat pasta and bread)

While these foods aren't a 100 percent cure-all for hormone dips, they'll definitely help keep the big mood plummets at bay. And they'll also allow you to feel more in control of your body, freeing you up to focus on your DD and adjust to your challenging new role as Mama in Chief.

rewrite the new-mom script

Newsflash: "Good" mothers come in all shapes and sizes, with as many personality twists and turns as there are grains of sand on Waikiki Beach. But if there is one common denominator—and I feel in my still slightly poochy gut that there is—it's a loving spirit. Easy, you say? Not when I up the ante by demanding you apply that loving spirit not only to your to unspeakably adorable new bébé, but to yourself, too.

the**mother**load

"When I first got home from the hospital with my son, I cried all the time! My older sister, who had a two-year-old at the time, gave him his first bath while my husband and I watched, since we were both clueless and nervous. I ended up calling my sister at least once a day to ask for help and sometimes just to cry because I didn't want to bother my husband at work. On some level, I knew all the tears were temporary and hormonal, but that didn't make it any easier. I definitely never laughed at myself because I was always so scared about doing everything 'wrong.' I couldn't see the humor in the bumps along the way. And sometimes I still feel like, 'When is this baby's real mom going to come get him?'"

—**Jill S.**, mama of two

"I'm either down on myself for not being more present for my kids or down on myself for neglecting my career," says Christine, mama of twins. "I can't win in that department. I constantly have to convince myself that I actually am a good mother. It's an endless source of stress, but I'm really working on it."

See what I mean about the evils of second-guessing yourself? With all she has on her plate, Christine, like so many other super-smart new mothers I know, is expending tons of much-needed energy on guilt tripping. What Christine may have needed—and you could probably benefit from, as well—is what I call a Mental Momover, a superconstructive new way of thinking about your postbaby life.

To the Rescue: A Mental Momover

A top-down, Mental Momover starts with ditching the pre-conceived notions of how "good" mothers juggle their new-mom responsibilities with everything else. By doing that, you'll create lots of new space for—*gasp*—trusting your own instincts. With so many parenting experts around these days, it's easy to start thinking that just about everyone knows more about this "mommy thing" than you do. But while these experts might know babies with a capital "B," they don't know *your* baby. And more important, they don't know *you*. Start with a clean slate and incorporate whatever tips and tricks work for your baby, your life, and you.

learn to love monotasking

The cornerstone of a Mental Momover—and this carries over to your upcoming Physical and Spiritual Momovers, too—is mastering the ability to focus on the task at hand, whether it's organizing the diaper bag so you can get out the door in a timely fashion or sitting still for ten minutes while you practice your meditation. I'll admit that I literally had to train myself not to bounce all over the place. But guess what? I did. Now, whenever I find myself ping-ponging at work or home—sorting the laundry for a few minutes then getting distracted by a pile of mail that needs opening and then deciding that what I *really, really* need to do at that precise moment is make myself a yummy pb&j on multigrain—I repeat my favorite mantra to myself: *Do what you're doing, Dana.* That's my little way of telling myself to finish what I start or face the consequences (e.g., a load of darks that never quite makes it into the washing machine, a mountain of junk mail and catalogs that lingers while I read the new *Time* magazine, and a kitchen countertop strewn with Skippy Natural and Smuckers jars).

Now, Do What You're Doing

I highly recommend pondering that simple little phrase—*Do what you're doing*—and applying it to your brand-new postbaby life. Just think of how much more joyful those early days could be if your sole focus was just navigating the next minute or hour. (Or if you're feeling especially energetic and ambitious, the whole day.) For the time being, put a ban on projecting into the distant future in that hyper, "Well, if I don't start her on the French flashcards *right now,* she'll never make it into the top 10 percent of her preschool class" way. Instead, think small and celebrate even seemingly minor achievements, à la: "It's nice out today. Maybe I'll nurse her on the porch" or "Yippee! I think I've finally got that swaddling technique down pat!"

You'll see; it's a huge relief to let go of all the planning, at least for now. Trust me, your scheduled-right-down-to-the-last-second life will still be there waiting once you and your baby exit your exquisite little postpartum cocoon. But by that point, you might be completely hooked on your new (healthier) roll-with-the-punches mindset.

worked for me!

Keeping a Self-Care Chart

Between the C-section, blood transfusion, and fact that I'd pretty much never even touched a baby before bringing my DD home from the hospital, I was a bit of a train wreck immediately postpartum. Still, I knew I needed to make a concerted effort to physically recuperate. So I did what I always do whenever an upsetting life situation throws my concentration off: I shifted into autopilot. I call it "going clipboard," and it entails making lots of to-do lists for myself until the mental fogginess lifts.

My Self-Care Chart was a postbaby riff on a to-do list, and its main function was to ensure that I was doing what I needed to do to get well. And here's why it was crucial: I was in pain from the C-section (duh), but refused to take the hardcore prescription meds because I didn't want to feel too out of it to care for the tot. Instead, I opted for Extra-Strength Tylenol, and plenty of it. There was just one problem: I couldn't remember when I'd taken the last pill. So I started keeping a running tab, which quickly morphed into an entire chart that included water intake, meals, snacks, naps, the measly amounts of milk I was able to pump, etc. I even recorded the number of maxi pads I was soaking through each day just in case the ob-gyn asked for an update to gauge my level of post-op blood loss (which he did, by the way).

Though it might seem overwhelming at the time, I think all just-home-from-the-hospital moms should keep their own version of my geeky little chart. In my opinion, it serves several different purposes. One, if you're on pain meds—prescription or OTC—you need to make sure you're not exceeding recommended doses. Two, with a baby wailing at the top of her lungs, it's easy to blow off eating properly and drinking enough water, and a daily chart provides a quick assessment of where you stand on that front. Three, you're sending a message to yourself from day one that "Mom Matters," and nothing—*nothing*—is more important than that.

chapter•two

call in the troops

As former First Mama Bear, that über-smarty Hillary Clinton was completely onto something: it *does* take a village to raise our DDs. But now that we're firmly ensconced in the twenty-first century, the challenging part is cobbling together our own newfangled version of an old-fashioned baby-raising posse. Depending on your situation, you may have none, one, some, or all of the following ready and willing to pitch in and share diaper duty: hubby or life partner; family; and/or a pack of pals who actually come through in a pinch.

But even if your stash of mother's helpers is a little sparse, here's what's completely cool about the nonvillage-y times we're living in: An extra set of hands—as well as entire cyber-communities of new moms just like you—is often just a mouse click away.

guilt is so last century

Of course, knowing how to find help and actually asking for it are two very different things. I don't know when we women latched onto the cockamamie notion that we're supposed to have stellar careers and then also tackle everything home-related by ourselves, but it kind of sucks. Add a helpless infant to the equation and driven, overachieving new mothers are headed for burnout.

Patricia, mama of twins who were born seven weeks early, had an especially tough time reaching out for the extra help she desperately needed. "I don't recall getting many offers—everyone was just so busy with their own lives and kids," she says. "However, I also didn't ask. I felt funny asking, mostly because I didn't want people to have to reject me. I knew how horribly exhausting and boring those early days were, so I figured no one else would want to go through that either. When I think back on that, that was so dumb!"

For the record, Patricia is so very *not* dumb. And thankfully, she at least let adult members of her own household pitch in. "I was very clear that I wasn't Superwoman," she says. "I would nudge my husband awake when it was his turn to feed a baby. And I would ask my mother-in-law, who lived with us for part of the year, to watch them while I ran to Starbucks for ten minutes. I still remember the joy and relief at walking out the door unencumbered by babies or all that gear."

Obviously, all the stuff that makes us great mama material—a take-charge attitude, an ability to blast through a mind-warpingly massive to-do list on a daily basis, is also what stops us from waving the little white flag when we really need to. "There are a lot of moms who are what I call 'CEOs of the Household,'" says Vanessa Wauchope, founder of Sensible Sitters, a babysitting and nanny-placement agency serving families in New York, LA, and Palm Beach. "They excel at everything at work, and they're determined to excel at everything at home too, right down to the bottles, the diapers, and the feedings. So it's a really big hurdle for them to ask someone to come in and help."

My tough-love recommendation? Get over it. You'll be doing everyone—your baby, hubby, and you—a massive favor if you mothball your Wonder Woman costume and ship it off to the attic for a spell. You can always break it back out on occasion for a trip down what-was-I-thinking memory lane and a hearty chuckle.

grab those helping hands

Tug your ear if you've ever offered to help someone and secretly hoped they wouldn't take you up on it. I knew it; every person alive has done that at least once. But for every time you've faked it, I'll also bet that there were ten other instances when you were completely ready to step up to the plate.

Taking care of a newborn is a different level of hard; we're talking Tour de France hard. Don't make it infinitely more difficult by refusing to accept the aid that's offered to you. If it makes you feel better, you can make a solemn promise to return the favor or at least buy your friend a really gorgeous Hermès scarf or a beautiful pair of earrings. Besides, a lot of times, allowing someone to help out is super bonding. Though both my own parents and my hubby's are no longer living, we each have a million siblings. And about six weeks after I delivered, my sister Jan arrived for a week. That added up to three clueless adults passing the baby around like a bawling little hot potato.

But it was actually really fun. We just ordered in all our meals, watched *Oprah* every afternoon and *Nip/Tuck* on DVD at night, and laughed our sleep-deprived heads off.

reserve the right to . . .

. . . hang a "Do Not Disturb" sign on your bedroom door, even when your mother-in-law or dear old Aunt Bessie is pitching in to help with the baby. Sure, the first time might feel a bit awkward, perhaps even a little rude, but you'll get used to it. Better yet, so will they.

Though most help happens after delivery, twins mama Christine was lucky enough to have her parents on hand before *and* after. "The week before was *amazing*," she recalls. "First, I had a few things left on the to-do list and I had been on house arrest (modified bed rest) for weeks by that point. And second, I loved having that predelivery moral support. It's a freaky thing to know that in a matter of days you'll have two more family members and my parents were a big help." Shortly after her folks left, Christine's mother-in-law arrived and "cooked up a storm. She stocked our freezer with amazing meals, which we ate for months."

A very independent type, Christine concedes that the arrival of twins, rather than one tiny tot, made it easier to just give in to the assistance gods. "I couldn't afford to say no to help," she says. "If I had had just one baby, I probably would have tried to do everything myself. It's completely my personality to say 'I can handle it,' when this is exactly the time we should be accepting help from any willing body." *Exactly.*

build your network

After you've tapped out the family tree and solicited help from every relative from your very own mama and in-laws to fourth cousins twice removed, you'll probably need (and hopefully want) to start relying on the kindness of strangers. Yes, you read that right: people you don't actually know.

You can probably sense that when it comes to my own DD, I'm the opposite of a control freak. Which isn't to say that I'm especially laid back. And it *definitely* doesn't mean that I'm lazy. (Let's put it this way: I have a full-time job and I squeezed the writing of this book into early mornings, late nights, and bits and pieces of weekend. And not that I'm bragging or anything, but I managed to read *Anna Karenina,* all 935 pages of it, in my "spare" time.) Rather, it just means that I realized pretty quickly—as in day one kind of quickly—that I was out of my league on the infant front. I had zero-zip-nada experience taking care of a baby. But as I soon discovered, there are plenty of people who've made babies their business, from nurses and nannies to services like Sensible Sitters and Sittercity.com, as well as gung-ho college kids whom you can track down through your church or local university. And I happily, and proudly, now employ a small fleet of 'em. My very own DIY village.

But perhaps you're the type who has a wee bit of trouble loosening the reins. That's cool, as long as you realize that your mental health would benefit big time if you did precisely that. "I understand that letting someone else in is a foreign concept," Wauchope says. "You already have this new little person running your life, and now you're letting a *stranger* give you advice?"

Look, I'm not saying I think you should just hand your tot off to the first person who happens by. Even I didn't do that. Instead, I signed up with Sensible Sitters, which screens every applicant to smithereens. Of course, lots of new moms might not have the financial means, or even the desire, to work with agencies. For those who want to do their own recon and interviewing, extensive due diligence can squelch the fears attached to hiring new people to take care of your precious little Pampers wearer. So, in addition to demanding recent references and making sure to actually call them (lots of people don't), Wauchope strongly advises touching on these three vital areas during the interview process:

- **The caregiver's experience with scheduling.** Are they comfortable adhering to your preferred meal and sleep schedules? Do they have experience establishing their own schedules for the children they've cared for previously?
- **The caregiver's nutritional values.** "Nutrition is really important," says Wauchope. Once your DD is onto solids, "if you want them to have homemade organic food, and the caregiver has no knowledge about that, or doesn't appreciate it, that's a big red flag. If somebody eats at McDonald's three times a day, you know they'll be bringing your child to McDonald's." Though I myself ate my fair share of Twinkies and Pop-Tarts® when I was a kid, I now see the folly in that. So for me, and hopefully for you, a penchant for junk is a real deal breaker.
- **The caregiver's long-term availability.** This is important, even if you're hiring someone just for a regular weekly date night with your hubby and your DD will likely be asleep for a good chunk of the time. "As a parent, you want to give yourself peace of mind," Wauchope says. "So it's really important for someone to know the bedtime routine. When she walks in, it needs to be seamless—she should know where the stuffed animal is, know what books to read. And later on, think about it from the older child's perspective: Is it better for her to have a new face every time or for her to know, 'Oh, Jackie's coming, and she's really fun'?"

I say, give Grandmama a night off and let the experts do their stuff, at least once in a while. If you can mentally crack the door open enough to let other nonfamily caregivers in, there's frequently a big payoff: objective counsel from individuals who've handled way more kids than you. "As helpful as a mother or mother-in-law is," says Wauchope, "it's sometimes easier to digest advice from someone who is completely detached from your family." All that and a much-needed night out, too? What are you waiting for? Pop open that cell phone and start booking.

join the crowd(s): new-mom support groups

Sometimes I'm convinced I have a split personality. I've picked a very "public" line of work (as an on-staff editor at a high-profile fashion magazine) and I have a solid crew of besties that I try to see as much as possible. However, the idea of throwing myself into a room with a bunch of women I don't know makes me feel like the shy kid hiding behind the monkey bars at recess.

the**mother**load

"I didn't stick with a new-mom group in a formal way, but a few of us came together when my son was between three and six months old and it was huge savior for me. Although some of us were from the original new-moms group, others were from a baby-gym class or were introduced through friends. We asked each other questions, commiserated over various things—it was wonderful. In fact, we still get together for monthly ladies' nights, eight years later!"

—**Elizabeth**, mama of two

While it certainly isn't too late for me to join a new-mothers group, I sort of regret not doing it earlier. And I'm not alone in that sentiment. "I didn't join any new-mom support groups because I didn't quite understand their value," says mama Mara. "I would just call my mother whenever questions would come up. But as time marched on, I realized that although my mom generally knew best, a lot of progress and changes in thinking about child care and development had been made, making her advice well-meaning but sometimes outdated. So I tended to hit my books and trusted websites for answers. A playground full of like-minded moms could have been just the thing."

Keep in mind that you can always shape your participation in new-mom groups to fit your own needs. In fact, sometimes just dipping a toe into a new network can yield benefits, per mama Christine, who joined a group for parents of multiples after she had her twins. "I didn't participate in any events with the group until my kids were older," she says, "but I did read the e-mail messages sent back and forth between twin and triplet moms who were asking for—and doling out—advice. I found that very helpful."

I hope I've convinced you of the value of letting others pitch in with caring for Baby. If you've had a long-standing issue with asking for help—one that predates the arrival of your DD—it may take some time before you become really proficient at it. But I really think you'll find "sharing the wealth" (or at least the nappy changes!) to be invaluable in helping you achieve balance and regain your sense of self, which you'll learn more about in the next chapter.

worked for me!

Hiring a Baby Nurse

When I look back, it all seems very *Mary Poppins*, happy ending and all, but it certainly didn't start out that way. Although Hubby and I had booked a baby nurse months before I was scheduled to deliver, she canceled the day before I was to be released from the hospital. Pushing the panic button, Hubby nabbed a list of nanny agencies from Command Central in the maternity ward and started dialing. Within a few hours, he'd secured a replacement nurse, a take-charge type named Grace who was available to dive in just two days after we'd brought our bawling bundle home.

From the get-go, Grace was full of opinions and advice that she had absolutely no qualms dispensing. Her first order of business was to offer up her sister Merle to take over when her two-week stint with us was up. (Suffice it to say that Grace is very in demand, and glides seamlessly, coast to coast, from one freaked-out household to the next.) Of course, there were other matters Grace weighed in on, too, from insisting I drink a nightly beer to improve my milk production (a Trinidadian wives' tale, me thinks, but fun nonetheless) to the necessity of excavating the poor DD's tiny, stuffed-up little nose with one of those terrifying bulb-shaped snot-extractor thingamajigs.

Along with shepherding us through that wildly clueless time, it was Grace's proffering of her little sis Merle that was the real life changer. We ended up keeping Merle for seven months extra-full-time (meaning she lived with us) before we finally weaned ourselves enough to hire a nine-to-five, Monday through Friday nanny.

Even then we "cheated" by having Merle around on weekends until the baby celebrated her first birthday. Yes, it was indulgent—and expensive—but it was a decision we definitely don't regret. By the time we finally waved buh-bye to our baby nurse, our DD was taking her very first steps.

And in so many ways, so were we.

baby step into your brand-new life

L et's just say, for argument's sake, that you've led a fairly typical American life prior to giving birth, complete with four years of college followed by stints as a single and a head-over-heels newlywed. With all that under your belt, at the very least, you've racked up a good twenty-five baby-free years.

My point is that you've had a hell of a lot more time on your own than you've had with your wee one. So why would you expect to be a just-add-water expert on all things Baby? Putting that kind of pressure on yourself is a prescription for misery. And misery, as I trust you've gleaned by now, is not part of the Momover equation.

Feeling *your* way, making it up as you go along, trusting that your basic mama instincts will consistently lead you to the right choices for you and your tot—now that's more like it. And if you can also manage to consciously, deliberately squeeze a little fun into your days, I solemnly promise that a year from now you'll be blown away at how much you've learned and how many joyful moments have piled up between nappy changes.

blended idea: little baby, little you, whole lotta new stuff

Pre-DD, I'm almost certain that "child free" wasn't the first phrase you used to describe yourself. Instead, your little rap, trotted out at job interviews or cocktail parties, probably included identifiers like "triathlete" or "Yale graduate" or "critical-care nurse" or "Scrabble addict." Depending on who was doing the listening, you might have tossed "married" or "single" into the mix.

As soon as a tot enters the picture, especially if it's your first, the "new mom" signifier becomes a huge, massive, gigantic part of your identity. In fact, it pretty much capsizes everything else for a while. It's all you can think about and the first thing that flies out of your mouth if you run into an old acquaintance who hasn't seen you in a while. But then something miraculous happens: You start to feel you creeping back into the picture. Every conversation doesn't begin and end with some anecdote about the baby. In fact, you can actually form entire sentences that don't include the words "feedings," "diapers," and "naps."

According to Bria Simpson, author of *The Balanced Mom*, it's superhealthy to start shifting at least a little of the focus away from your precious tot. "We're in a child-centered culture right now and it feels 'normal' to be baby-obsessed and 'abnormal' to be more family balanced, where Mom and Dad are also a priority," she says. "But at some point, most mothers who micromommy and lose themselves in their children will have a gnawing sense that something isn't quite right. Then they either choose to ignore that void within them, often by keeping a very hectic schedule, shopping, playing lots of tennis, volunteering, etc. Or they make the decision that they want their identities back."

the**mother**load

"I just took a sculpting class at the Art Students League. I'm a creative person and I knew it would fulfill a need I have for creative stimulation. I felt very guilty the night before the course started, but after a few minutes the guilt went away and pure bliss took over. I think it's my job to show my kids how to live a full life, and that it's okay to improve and take time to grow as a person. The more stimulation and growing I do, the better equipped I am to parent. And there's no way for that to happen if I'm not mixing in different circles."

—Rebekah, mama of two

Of course, you may have given birth so recently that the notion of drifting through the mall in search of new stilettos or whacking a tennis ball around seems like a distant memory; all the fun stuff you'll never get back to again. But trust me, you will. And the sooner you realize that it's perfectly okay not to define yourself 100 percent by your new motherhood, the happier you'll be.

establish a few ground rules

In theory, they sound like a big old drag, but you know what's great about systems and routines? Once you've got them down, you can sort of go on autopilot and zone out—a massive blessing for a sleep-deprived mama bear.

So, if you follow none of the other recommendations in this book, promise me you'll whip up your own personal new-mom constitution. Granted, I'm writing mine in hindsight, but here's the credo I wish I'd set for myself the second my DD decided to finally join us:

- I will diligently treat myself with as much care as I do the baby, mentally, physically, and spiritually.
- I will cut myself major slack for the newborn stuff I don't know, and I will celebrate and reward myself for all the progress I'm making with a super-splurgy new handbag.
- I will blame hormones for 99 percent of any bad feelings I might be having.
- I will build at least one (and preferably many, many more) mommy time-outs into my day, including reading snippets of a million delicious Edith Wharton novels and steeping in steaming-hot aromatherapy baths.
- I will eat well because it makes me feel great, but I will not freak out if I occasionally fall off the good-food wagon.
- I will recognize that, a year from now, I won't even remember most of the nonsense I'm fretting over and obsessing about.

figure out what's working; toss what isn't

In the forty-week preamble to delivery, most of us, especially the first timers who don't have older kids underfoot, had a little free time to build our perfect-mommy expectation level about as high the top of the Eiffel Tower. Maybe you were determined to use cloth diapers or make your own 100 percent organic baby food or start breaking out the Mandarin and French flashcards the second your newborn was able to focus her blurry little eyes.

Some of my early strategies proved smart, like my decision to forego pacifiers. In my first few weeks at *Cookie*, I edited a Q&A on the pros and cons of binky use. And one of the big "take-aways" from the piece, for me at least, was the difficulty in eventually weaning toddlers off the little hunks of rubbery plastic. Although pediatrician Cara Natterson, whose expert opinion we tapped, offered the most adorable tough-love schemes for breaking the addiction (including rounding them all up and pretending to mail them to a "baby who really needs them"), I figured it might be better not to introduce them in the first place. Still, I nabbed a freebie from the giveaway table at the office and, on the DD's first night home from the hospital, I slipped it into her mouth. But I was so alarmed at the Freddy Kruegerish hockey-mask effect on my sweet tot's tiny face that I tossed it and haven't used one since.

A far tougher decision was to bail on not only breastfeeding, but pumping milk as well. From the start, perhaps because I was in such rough physical shape myself, the breastfeeding thing just wasn't coming together in the hospital. But having taken that beyond-crunchy labor-prep class I referred to earlier, I was absolutely determined that under no circumstances would baby formula cross my daughter's lips. Thankfully, the maternity ward nurses could recognize a hungry newborn when they saw one, and I remember sobbing bitterly when they insisted that we augment my measly offerings with something more substantial.

When we all returned home, I started pumping like a crazed lunatic. Locked in the bathroom with my spanking new $300 dual-boob contraption, I'd diligently hammer away and pop out, twenty minutes later, with maybe an ounce of mama's milk to feed my seven-pound, eleven-ounce DD. Of course, the entire time we were also feeding her formula; my daughter wouldn't be here today if I'd been vain and stubborn enough to stick to my mother's-milk guns. About a month into my determined pumping regime, I came to my senses and kicked the whole kit and caboodle to the curb. If only my feelings of failure had been as easy to get rid of.

But in true Momover spirit, I'm now every bit as intent on losing that negativity as I was on eking out a lousy drop of milk from my raw, aching nipples. Do I wish I had been able to breastfeed my daughter? Absolutely. The few times I did, it was insanely bonding. But as I watch her today, at three years of age and fussing around with her Barbie karaoke machine in her cheerful, toy-stuffed bedroom, I know that she's healthy, strong, and perfectly fine. And I'm willing to bet that whatever similar choices you've made on the ditching-perfection front have turned out just as well.

reserve the right to . . .

. . . exchange a small mountain of baby presents for something really gorgeous just for you. I can virtually guarantee that your little bundle of joy doesn't really need fifteen impossibly gorgeous hand-loomed blankies. You, on the other hand, just might be in the market for a cozy new cashmere sweater or shawl. Why shouldn't you both be wrapped up in something yummy?

reconnect with the outside world on your own terms

By now, you're already realizing that one of the key themes of this book is that there isn't a one-size-fits-all new-mom template. For every one of you who is climbing the walls in anticipation of getting back into the social swing, there's another new mom who just wants to hang out and hibernate with the baby for a while longer.

"I tried like hell to see friends in the early months, but honestly I think my twins were seven or eight months old before I really felt like a human being again," says mama Christine. "I was distracted and very one-track minded and, to be honest, I was really aware of not boring my friends to death with new baby stories. So I felt a little self-conscious when I spent time with people; it's all I wanted to talk about but I felt like I had to hold back."

Jill S. says it took her a full six months after delivering before she felt like heading from her home in the 'burbs to New York to visit with pals. "Even then, I was feeling guilty for not being home with my son, and then feeling ridiculous for feeling guilty," she says. "I went away for one night when he was ten months old, leaving him with my husband. I ended up coming home early!"

However, other new moms were itching to return to some semblance of their old social life. After two months of bed rest leading up to the delivery of her twins, mama Jenny R. got back into circulation almost immediately. "As soon I could go—probably two weeks after they were born—I started to meet friends," she says. "Maybe with one child I might have felt guilty about that. But having two was so overwhelming that I really liked getting out of the house for a bit." And oh-so smartly, she did.

Wherever you fall on the spectrum of socializing mamas—whether you're naturally the life of the party or a little shy—tune in to what you really feel up for. Learn to trust your inner voice, and be sure to rest up. You'll need some get up and go for Part 2: Getting It Together Physically.

Penciling in My Pals

Before my DD arrived on the scene, I'd long enjoyed a completely festive social life. I've lived in the same city since college (a huge one, New
York), shacked up in a few summer houses in the Hamptons, and had
a long career at a handful of great magazines. When I add that all up,
I've amassed a group of deeply excellent buddies. I'm not one of those
monster networkers with 5,000 Facebook friends, but I absolutely cher-
ish the pals I do have. And there was no way I was letting them go just
because I became a mama.

Perhaps hard-driving Gotham is to blame, but a good chunk of my
closest friends don't have kids—several aren't even married. But since I
was determined to stay in touch regardless of our now-different life-
styles, I made the executive decision to just put on my single-girl hat
when we hung out. Which doesn't mean I flirted with the hot guy at the
next table or downed more than a glass or two of Champs. I just kept
the baby talk to a minimum, and I didn't whip out the adorable pictures
unless I was asked.

Instead, I did what I've always done: connect. Ideally, that connection
took place face to face. I'd rather see someone every few months and
really talk than exchange a lot of surface e-mails. So, even though I now
had a million new infant-related things going on in my life, I was never
the one to cancel dinner or drinks.

Granted, this was all coming from a really selfish place; I always feel
about 1,000 percent better about virtually everything in my life when I
keep my pals in the loop, and I also want to know what's happening in
their lives.

Not that I didn't go through a hunkering-down period right after
delivering. But as soon as I felt up to it, I started making plans. Over the

years, my friends and I have helped each other through rough patches and whooped it up during the good times. That kind of support isn't something I'd ever let go of. In fact, I'm convinced it will even make me a better mother.

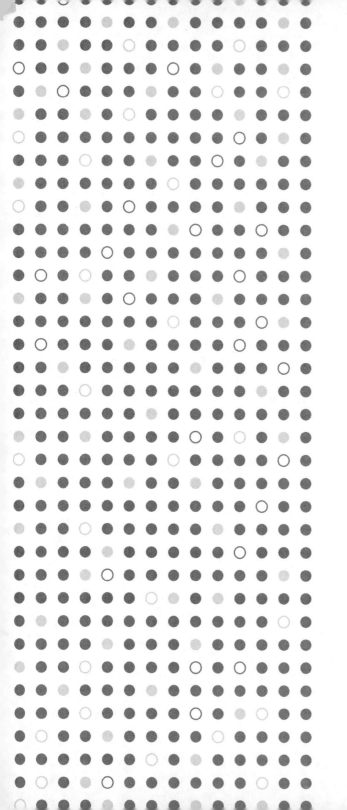

getting it together
physically

I don't need to tell you how much your body has changed in the past year; one quick peek at your naked self in a full-length mirror will do the trick on that front. But what I am going to share in the upcoming chapters are about a million ways to safely, sanely, and naturally get your prebaby body back. Now that you have your head on straight (thanks to your Mental Momover), it's time to put yourself on the path to wellness. That includes keeping up to date on your important medical tests, easing back into exercise (and then really going for it), and rediscovering the magical powers of a dash of lipstick or spritz of perfume. Oh, and maybe a really great push-up bra. . . .

chapter•four

checkups: one for baby, one for you

When your baby was still an inside job, tucked deep in your blossoming belly, all those visits to the ob-gyn were at least partially about you. Sure, the tot's progress was crucial, particularly once the little cutie started to gain steam and fill out a bit in there, but—and this is probably especially true if you were a first timer and not a seasoned baby machine—how you were faring during the pregnancy, physically and mentally, was also part of the agenda.

Once everyone's safely home from the hospital, however, it's a very different story. At that point, you'll be taking your DD to the pediatrician so often you'll seriously consider building an underground tunnel. Every month, you'll bundle up your little bundle of joy and motor off for a little look-see. And that doesn't include all the extra trips you'll be taking at the slightest sign of a cough, sniffle, or earache. So what's in it for you?

what's up, doc

Between the pregnancy and the newborn period, you've wracked up a lot of frequent flier miles on the doc front, but you still need to keep going. Why? Because with so much going on in Baby Town, it's incredibly easy to blow off medical care for yourself. And now, perhaps more than ever, your health is *muy importante*. How can you expect to take primo care of the baby if you're not feeling 100 percent? So, not only do I want you to keep up to speed on all the important screening tests (and to facilitate that, I've provided a chart for you below), I want you to head off to whatever specialist you need to see at the mere hint of a real medical issue.

I don't want you to do this in a paranoid, freaked-out way. But in a take-charge, level-headed "Mom-Matters" way. Health problems have a nice little way of disappearing if they're dealt with sooner rather than later. So I urge you to step up to the plate, book the appointment, hire a sitter or enlist a family member or pal to mind the wee one, and get your ass to the doctor. Now!

my own personal wake-up call

Pinkie-swear: This is my last scary Dana story. But again, as with my post–C-section blood-transfusion tale, I think you'll find it helpful.

And if it motivates even one of you new mama bears to pick up the phone and dial your doc, it will have served its purpose.

When my little lady was about eighteen months old, I popped by my dermatologist's office for some sprucing up. Specifically, I was in the market for a light chemical peel to "brighten" my skin, one of my few doctor-administered beautifiers. (Highly recommended, by the way, especially when augmented with the DIY version; we'll get to that in the all-important "primping" chapter.)

In addition to the peel, I was also hoping the derm could determine the cause of an annoying flaky patch on my forehead, which had been appearing and disappearing for a few weeks by that point. Though I thought it was probably just a little eczema, my doctor knew immediately that it wasn't and ordered a biopsy. Unfortunately, she was right; as it turns out, it was an *actinic keratosis*, a precursor to skin cancer. And here I'd thought that it was only morphing moles that needed to be monitored. . . .

After that scare, you'd think I'd get a baseline melanoma screening, right? Wrong. It didn't even occur to me, and this was after decades as a beauty editor, a profession in which a big part of the job description is to attend all manner of ghoulish presentations on skin cancer. Nope, I was forty-five years old and had never had a skin-cancer screening. Did I also mention the fact that I'm blond, blue eyed, fair skinned, and had baked in the sun like a brownie for eons?

Long story short: When I finally returned to the derm the following year for another chemical peel, she insisted on a quick full-body scan. This time, seven (!) biopsies were ordered. Of those seven, only one was completely benign. The rest contained abnormal tissue and had to be dealt with accordingly. I'm unspeakably relieved that my doctor caught everything early, but let's be honest here—had I not been prompted by sheer vanity to waddle off to a skin specialist for a little cosmetic tune-up, I may have been staring down the Big "C" before long.

Here's the happy ending: I'm ultravigilant now, and get regular head-to-toe screenings alongside my own monthly self-checks. More important, I've learned the value of preventive care. I know that by catching a dodgy-looking mole or a flaky patch in its initial stages, my chances of nipping a potentially serious problem in the bud are much, much greater. For example, my eye doctor has determined that I have an enlarged optical nerve. Should that eventually lead to the initial stages of glaucoma (and of course I'm keeping my fingers crossed that it won't), we'll be able to pounce on it and treat it immediately, thereby staving off potential vision loss.

prioritizing your health

By now, you know that the whole point of a Momover is to take excellent care of yourself mentally, physically, and spiritually. But how you achieve that core goal is constantly changing. For the early postpartum period, taking the very best care of yourself might mean ordering seven pairs of the same cozy sweatpants online and refusing to wear anything else for those first few weeks. Later on, it could encompass getting serious about that residual belly blubber by keeping a food log and hitting the gym more frequently. Still further into your new-mom journey, learning to meditate could move to the top of your stress-reduction to-do list.

All of those steps are incredibly positive, but for the most part they're solo activities, the important stuff you do for yourself, by yourself. In order to stay megahealthy, you need to partner with the best medical professionals you can find. Then you need to kick it up a few notches by:

- Keeping current with all necessary screening exams
- Following the recommendations of your doctors, as long as they make perfect sense to you, and seeking a second opinion if they don't

- Identifying a few reputable information resources that serve as your go-to knowledge base for staying abreast of the ever-changing health field

reserve the right to . . .

. . . bring a long list of questions, comments, and concerns with you to your annual physical and ask to spend a few minutes reviewing your medical chart. In this era of warp-speed doctor's visits, it's in your best interest to be proactive.

That last point is critical. Every day, it seems the results of a new study on women's health issues are released. That's why it's crucial to track down media "filters" you trust. As a health journalist and recovering cyberchondriac, I've explored countless news sources, some infinitely better than others. I've listed my favorites in the Dig Deeper Appendix.

Knowledge is power. So stay tuned in to the nuances of your own health, including any postbaby changes such as fatigue that linger beyond six months. Also be sure to book the following exams on the recommended schedule.

The Biggies: Tests You Absolutely Cannot Skip

After your six-week postpartum checkup, which will include a pelvic exam and Pap test, you'll need to get back to routine (read: nonpreggo) health maintenance. These tests will give you the big picture, but be forewarned, this is a comprehensive checklist that covers everything, including tests such as a colonoscopy, which you may be too young for.

Test Name	Frequency	Check ✔
Blood glucose	Baseline at age forty-five; every three years thereafter	
Blood pressure	At least every two years	
Cholesterol	Frequency at recommendation of primary care physician; norm is a baseline screening at age twenty, then at least every five years thereafter	
Clinical breast exam	Every two years between age twenty and forty; yearly thereafter, augmented by monthly self-exam	
Colonoscopy	Baseline at age fifty, then every ten years thereafter	
Dental exam and cleaning	Twice yearly (yup, every six months; more and more research points to the link between oral health and overall body health)	
Eye exam	Yearly	
Mammogram	Baseline at age forty (earlier if you have a family history of breast cancer), then every one or two years	
Pap test and pelvic exam	Yearly	

Test Name	Frequency	Check ✔
Skin exam	Yearly, augmented by monthly self-exam	
Physical	Yearly	
TSH (Thyroid Stimulating Hormone)	Baseline at age thirty-five, every five years thereafter	

Above and Beyond: Other Screenings to Consider

In the interest of health, you could spend every waking minute—not to mention a small fortune—running from clinic to clinic, health guru to health guru, testing this, that, or the other body part. And believe me, when I've been in the throes of intense cyberchondria or in the midst of my skin-cancer scare, I've considered doing precisely that. But at least until I'm a little older, I've decided to keep a lid on it. My goal now is to raise my game, testwise, without creating a whole new miniobsession.

the**mother**load

"I've always been fastidious about my own health care—teeth cleaned two or three times a year, annual mammogram, yearly visit to the gyno. If I don't feel well, I address the problem as quickly as I can. My biggest concern is being healthy for my children. I had my son at forty and my daughter at forty-three. This year I'll turn fifty, and now that I have kids, I want to live to 100. I want to see them grow up and have families of their own."

—**Gwen**, mama of two

To that end, I asked Jeffrey Morrison, MD, a New York–based medical doctor who specializes in nutrition (for more on his practice see the Dig Deeper Appendix), to compile a short list of the tests he thinks are crucial for all new moms. What's great is that, with the exception of the kidney function test, which entails forking over a cup of pee, each of these tests is conducted via blood sample. A vial or two of the red stuff and *voila,* access to all the personal data Dr. Morrison says we should arm ourselves with to stay healthy.

"We all need to be proactive," says Dr. Morrison. "So definitely get these baseline tests, which are the minimum that I would recommend. Then, based on what's going on in your life, and what we see on your original test, we can take the next step, if necessary."

So here's your cheat sheet for extra-credit new-mama health, complete with the rationale behind each test:

- **Complete blood count:** Among other things, measures amounts of white blood cells, red blood cells, and platelets. Can uncover immune-system issues as well as anemia, a common postpartum health woe.
- **Ferritin:** Checks level of ferritin, a protein in the body that binds to iron; can also uncover anemia.
- **Kidney function:** Determines whether the kidneys, which perform several vital tasks including removing waste from blood, balancing pH levels, and regulating internal water levels, are performing optimally.
- **Liver panel:** Consisting of seven tests run on the same blood sample; used to detect liver disease and assess overall liver health; often ordered for symptoms of fatigue.
- **Vitamin D:** Used to detect bone weakness as well as monitor diseases such as Crohn's and cystic fibrosis, which can obstruct the absorption of fat.
- **Vitamin B 12 and Folic Acid:** Can uncover anemia and nutritional deficiencies.

relax, you're fine

Basically, I want it both ways. While I insist that you move your own health to the top of the priority heap, keep up with all the standard maintenance screenings, and add a slew of other tests to the mix, I also don't want you to become *too* dialed in. It's important to strike a balance between having your head in the sand about what's going on with you physically and becoming a big old drama queen. I've done both, and I can tell you that neither extreme is a great place to be.

Unfortunately for mama Jeanine, she's morphed into a total hypochondriac since having her two boys. So for her, going to the doctor too much is a bigger problem than not going enough. "I find I'm more focused on death than ever before," she confides. "With every ache and pain I feel, I'm convinced it's cancer. And then I lie awake at night hoping I won't die before I'm at an age when they can remember Mommy. So I find myself going to the doctor for every small ailment."

Having a kid later in life really ups the ante on the worrying-about-mortality front. But because I'm so committed to getting a grip on my situational health anxiety—I say situational because it only surfaces when the word "biopsy" starts getting bandied about—I haven't included any of the big medical reference books in the Dig Deeper Appendix. Instead, I'm recommending another wildly popular tome (one of those big "You" books by docs Michael Roizen and Mehmet Oz), but one I feel is a lot more mental-health friendly.

By the way, if you think you might be tipping over into serious health-anxiety territory, I urge you to visit *www.healthanxiety.homestead.com*, the website of a recovering hypochondriac. She's been asymptomatic for years, but still maintains her site, which is filled with links, recommended reading, and her own poignant recovery tale, as a help to those in need. Hopefully, you're not one of them.

Although partnering with a trusted crew of medical experts is crucial for every new mama, it's only one piece of the total wellness puzzle. Another is getting moving again. If you're feeling okay and your doctor has given you the go-ahead, it's time to track down your workout gear. But don't fret, it's all about baby steps.

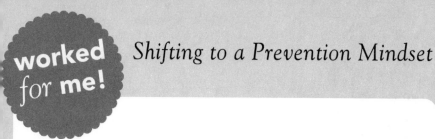

Shifting to a Prevention Mindset

During my second skin-cancer scare, while I waited for the results of all those gnarly biopsies to come back, I did so much reading I'm surprised my head didn't explode. Although slipping into denial mode would definitely have been easier on my psyche, at that time, that approach just wasn't an option. (It is now, happily; I've made tons of progress in eradicating my worst-case scenario thinking, which I'll share with you later in Chapter 13.) Instead, I devoured every shred of cancer-related information I could get my mitts on, with a subfocus on melanoma. Nothing too on the fringe, though; I stuck to reliable sources and steered clear of the countless "cancer cures" on the old Misinformation Superhighway.

While thankfully I didn't have melanoma or either of the other two, less deadly types of skin cancer (basal cell carcinoma or squamous cell carcinoma), I wasn't completely in the clear. A few of the biopsied areas had to be scraped a second time to make sure all the abnormal tissue was removed. And my derm and I are now on permanent high alert.

Still, I'm super optimistic for two reasons: One, I'll never skip another important screening exam, so I'll be much more likely to nip a potential problem in the bud. Two, all my reading has led me to believe that there are steps I can take, both big and small, to boost my overall health and strengthen my immune system. Though many are covered in-depth in upcoming chapters, here's my big-picture plan for staying healthy:

- Keeping stress under control with conscious anxiety management and focused relaxation—i.e., meditation
- Exercising regularly, even if on "light" days that just means a twenty-minute walk
- Maintaining a primarily vegetarian, heavily organic, diet

- Avoiding foods and beverages with tons of chemicals
- Wedging little "health hits" into my day, like sprinkling antioxidant-rich cinnamon and flaxseeds on my plain lowfat yogurt and squeezing pH-balancing lemons and limes into my filtered water
- Limiting sun exposure
- Hitting the hay early (on most nights, it's lights out by 10:00 P.M.)

chapter•five

the six-month window (tapping ma nature's get-back-in-shape help)

Right after you have a baby, at least for the first six weeks or so, your sole goals should be to slowly recover your strength and energy and bond with your delicious new DD. That's it, Mama. Sure, a few of you might feel up to the task of waddling around the neighborhood on a particularly gorgeous, sun-drenched afternoon, but if you're not, by all means, don't.

My little lady arrived in the dead of a New York winter, and I can assure you that apart from mandatory trips to the pediatrician, I rarely ventured outside of our cozy Battery Park City apartment. I can still remember what a huge deal it was for me, about ten days post–C-section, to brave a trek to the corner drugstore on my own. I had such a sense of accomplishment until my baby nurse laughed her head off at the giant plastic toddler bibs I proudly brought back home from my little shopping expedition. Oh well. How was I supposed to know the wee one wouldn't be able to use them for another year or so? At least I got a little fresh air for my efforts.

Mind you, I'm not advocating not moving a single muscle in those early weeks. As long as you've gotten the go-ahead from your ob-gyn, you can certainly do a few gentle stretches if you're up for it. And unless you enjoy finding small puddles of pee in your panties every time you laugh, cough, or sneeze, you'll be doing those godforsaken Kegels religiously. (Um, actually, they're kind of great for your sex life, too, so keep at 'em long after your tot is ambulatory.)

But once you're out of dazed-and-confused mode, it's time to go a little tough love on yourself. Or at least let me do it for you, because the sooner you start focusing your mind on getting back to your prebaby body (or some facsimile thereof), the more likely you are to actually achieve it. If you don't believe me, consider this info from the American College of Obstetricians and Gynecologists: Women who are still hanging on to the excess baggage acquired during pregnancy at the six-month mark are more likely to experience long-term obesity. And if you're planning subsequent babies, it's best to get a grip on this issue early.

By slowly inching out onto the physical-wellness ice, you can continue ramping up until you blast that baby blubber for good. To get you going, Mother Nature is standing by to provide some much-needed assistance.

shrink to fit: what happens immediately postdelivery

Although I was a cheerfully useless stoner in science class back in high school, I'm happy to report that I easily wrapped my mind around Postbaby Biology 101. That's because it's so basic: After you deliver, your body wants you to get back in shape. If it didn't, why would it work so hard to restore order around Casa Mama? Thanks to a special cocktail of postpartum hormones, your uterus begins to shrink within minutes of delivering and continues downsizing for approximately six weeks, at which time it will have virtually returned to its prepregnancy size. Water weight will have slipped off, too. And if you're nursing, you can also expect a slight jump in metabolism, enough to burn through up to 500 calories a day.

But before you start turning cartwheels about that extra caloric wiggle room, realize how quickly you can chew or sip your way through 500 calories. Let's just take a quick healthy snack as a guideline. By tucking into ½ cup of plain lowfat yogurt (about sixty calories), a handful of almonds (about 160 calories), one large banana (about 115 calories), and one cup of OJ (about 100 calories), you've just consumed 435 of those 500 calories. Hardly seems fair, right? Please know that I'm not trying to bum you out; I just want you to see how fast the calorie clock ticks, even for healthy, metabolism-boosting snacks like this one. So be vigilant and make that extra calorie hit work for you and your Momover.

psyching yourself up (and off that couch)

What's that old saying about objects at rest? Actually, it's Newton's First Law of Motion, aka "the law of inertia," and it basically posits that unless something major happens to upset the applecart, "bodies at rest"—and that would be you on the sofa with the remote and a box of Triscuits while your DD naps—aren't likely to budge. And who could blame you for wanting to stay put? You're exhausted. Every fiber of your being wants to stay welded to those comfy, crumb-filled cushions.

But let's just say there are other forces conspiring to keep you from exercising. Perhaps you're a neat freak like moi and you live for those random free minutes so you can tidy up, empty the dishwasher, change the kitty litter . . . the list is endless. But that's exactly the point: the list is endless. So, I'm begging you to drop the Swiffer, unplug the DustBuster, and prioritize your physical and mental health. Lowering your perfection standards until you get this new-mom thing under control is one of the best decisions you can make. You need to set a precedent ASAP, not later. It needs to be hardwired into your brain, à la, "I've just had a baby and I need to take extra-special care of myself, including getting some exercise, right now. End of story."

the**mother**load

"With my first child, I didn't go back to the gym until six months because that's when they allowed babies! It was my only break, and I really looked forward to it. I'm the type of person who is on again/off again with the gym, so I guess I just used the baby as an excuse not to go. But eight years, two kids, and three memberships later, I'm back at the gym and loving it. But I hate the fifteen minutes here, fifteen minutes there thing; I want to get in and have at least forty-five minutes to really sweat and feel like I've worked out. It's such a big stress reliever for me."

—**Elizabeth**, mama of two

Of course, that isn't to say that carving out time for our own needs is easy. "I think it's a mental discipline, and it's a choice that's really hard for most women," says Christina Attiken, founder of Momeez, a physical therapy company devoted to helping new mamas get back in alignment. "I find that a lot of my clients don't make themselves a priority at all, and if they miss that window, it's a hard road. It's definitely a critical period, and if they're not making that transition back into exercising and eating well, it becomes really difficult. The moms I work with early on are doing fine. But if I'm not seeing them in the first six months, they're working a lot harder."

even a little something trumps nothing

A super-successful friend of mine has a favorite expression: "Inch by inch, anything's a cinch." And while I've always loved this idea, I think it's especially perfect for a new mama to latch on to. One, it makes uphill battles (such as getting back in shape postdelivery) seem utterly doable. Two, at this stage of the game, who doesn't have an actual inch or two to tone and tighten?

Eventually you'll need and—wait for it—maybe even want to get back to a more comprehensive fitness program. But "eventually" isn't now; this is the training-wheels period, when you ease back into the game with little hits here and there, gradually extending the length of time you work out as your strength and energy rebound.

"New moms need to think of this time as a reclaiming of their bodies, because they've just gone through ten months of getting ready for Baby," says übertrainer David Kirsch, explaining his approach to helping scorching-hot mamas like Heidi Klum and Liv Tyler get back into shape after delivering. "And if you're nursing, you're limited on some level—you're not going to be able to go all out and do a hardcore boot camp or anything like that because your breasts are too big. You'll have to be a little kinder to your body. But assuming everything is fine, it's a pretty steady course. I find most postpregnant women are very motivated to feel sexy, to look great."

What Kirsch shares with fellow trainer La Reine Chabut—and virtually every other god- or goddess-like fitness guru I've had the good fortune to interview over the years—is an absolute, iron-clad, "no-excuses" policy. And as a busy mama of two and author of *Lose That Baby Fat,* Chabut has added insight into the special challenges posed by having a demanding newborn pulling you in about eighty different directions. While she's an advocate of starting early (as in as soon as your ob-gyn says it's okay kind of early), Chabut's all about what she calls "realistic fitness benchmarks" for the first postpartum year. A big component of this reality-check approach is slicing a workout into ten-minute chunks, five minutes on days when you're really crazed. By rewiring your brain a bit and losing the "all or nothing" mindset, Chabut says you can make real progress on the road back to your prebaby body.

In other words, every little bit counts. Just as each microscopic sliver of devil's food cake adds a devilish little half-inch to your behind (oh, the injustice of it all . . .), ten-minute blocks of time spent tightening, toning, and moving will begin to pile up in the hot-mama account. And just as important, you'll start to feel so motivated by your newfound stick-to-it-iveness, you'll be itching to step it up a notch. (Don't worry; we'll delve into "quickies" in-depth in Chapter 9.)

firing up your get-moving plan

When you think about Mother Nature's master plan, of course it makes perfect sense: In the immediate postpartum period, both mama and baby are both so shell-shocked that each party is (fingers and toes crossed) sleeping for big chunks of time. Then, by the time the DD starts to get her bearings, slowly mastering such feats of derring-do as clutching her rattle in a vise-like death grip, Mom has just enough energy to consider cranking out a few dozen Kegels or brave a walk around the block. As each day ticks by, the dynamic duo feels stronger and stronger.

If you're smart, and naturally you are, you'll maximize this momentum by gradually increasing your energy expenditure. In the first three months, this can be easily achieved by walking, either with or without the tot in tow. But don't just stroll willy-nilly; time yourself, police the number of steps you're taking with a pedometer, and for extra credit, consider using a heart monitor to ensure you're getting into your target zone.

In addition to making a concerted effort to walk, don't discount all the movement that's naturally built into your new-mama life. Attiken, for one, is convinced that new mothers get just as much exercise as some sweaty gym rat merely by going through the endless motions of their days. Hoisting your baby in and out of the crib and stroller and on and off the changing table is work (as if I even needed to tell you that). "New moms get more of a workout in a day than someone at a gym, in terms of burning calories and strengthening," she says. "They're lifting more weight than anyone else would."

For fun, you might want to clip your pedometer onto your sweats to see how many steps you're logging as you zoom around in your endless loop from the nursery to the kitchen to the bathroom to the living room and back to the nursery again. But be forewarned: Those little devices can be addictive. When I road tested a few a while back for one of my *Momover* columns, I wore it around the clock and even attached it to the bottom of my nightie because I wanted to record every single step I took. The goal was to try to beat my number from the previous day, and I started to get a little nutty about the whole thing, checking my count about a million times a day. But I suppose there are worse things in the world than trying to raise your game on the fitness front. Which brings me to my next point.

staying motivated

Remember way back in Chapter 1 when I talked about the importance of celebrating the little stuff, like learning how to swaddle? Well, it's even more important that you pat yourself on the back for attempting even the measliest morsel of exercise. Why? Because focusing on getting back in shape after having a baby has a long-range, big-picture impact on your physical and mental health. Not only does exercise lower your risk for all manner of illnesses from high blood pressure and Type 2 diabetes to certain forms of cancer, it is a tried-and-true stress buster. And I doubt there's a mama alive who doesn't have stress.

reserve the right to . . .

. . . wear your "skinny" jeans, provided you can zip them up, of course. Will you look great in them right now? Probably not. But if anyone can find me a better motivator for inching your way back into a postpartum fitness routine, I'm all ears.

In his inspiring book *Sound Mind, Sound Body*, Kirsch devotes plenty of ink to motivation as well as an entire chapter to what he describes as "getting a handle on your inner world," meaning the way you think about exercise and staying healthy. It's pretty deep, which I love, but one of the best tips is to stay focused on the present. None of this, "I'll start working out next week" or "next month" or "once the baby's in preschool" nonsense. This is your new life. Structure it with purpose.

Use whatever tricks you have up your sleeve to stay moving, even if it's merely the promise of a cookie or a half-cup of fro-yo for dessert. Personally, I find keeping a fitness log really motivating. I love looking at my little code: 2/27—30 min ellip/3.45/5, which translates into thirty minutes on the elliptical machine for a total of 3.45 miles at level five. Though I often fall short of the recommended fitness guidelines (as I write this, the U.S. Department of Health and Human Services is urging 150 minutes of moderate exercise and two strength-training sessions per week), I still work up a sweat on a regular basis. And there's something about seeing it all recorded for prosperity that makes me happy. Happy is good. Happy leads to perseverance and results. But of course you'll need real, lasting energy (not the fake-o, five-cups-of-coffee kind) to stay the course. So that's what the entire next chapter is devoted to—building your toolkit of healthy energizers.

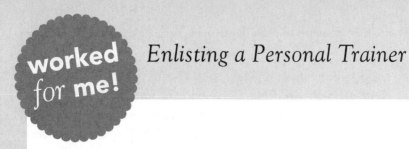

Enlisting a Personal Trainer

In hindsight, I guess I could've gotten my knickers in a twist. But I wasn't even remotely offended when Hubby handed me a gift certificate for a personal trainer before the DD was even born. Tucked inside my birth-day card, along with beaucoup mushy sentiments about our glorious future *en famille* (all of which came true, by the way), was a voucher for ten sessions with Sharon Jackson-Errico, a ripped woman who, oh so conveniently, happened to live in the same apartment building as us. As soon as I was up to it postbaby, I agreed to hit the gym and get to work.

In addition to being cut to smithereens, Sharon is also the same height as me—in the five-foot ballpark. So in a sense, she represents what I could look like if I buckled down (and/or quit my day job, gave the DD up for adoption, and logged, say, ten hours a day at the gym for a decade or so). Still, I made it my business not to be intimidated by this walking, talking paragon of self-discipline. Instead, I chose to push myself and reap the benefits of her wisdom.

Luckily, I'd worked out pretty consistently during my pregnancy, slogging away on that elliptical machine as my belly expanded to epic proportions. And, per doctor's orders, I really didn't eat everything that wasn't nailed down, so there wasn't a lot of actual weight to lose. Still, my postpartum midsection was shaking like a bowl full of jelly, and I had plenty of ground to recover on the feel-great front. So, through lots of weight work (gag) and old-school calisthenics (double gag), I slowly started to peel off some of that baby mush and recoup some energy.

In total, I met with Sharon thirty times, which proved to be just enough for me to get back into "fitness head." Forget the thinner thighs; the fact that Sharon made me actually want to exercise was worth more than all the tea in China. Because with a hell of an excuse not to hit the gym now toddling around the house asking if I'd like to play dolls with her, I'll take every ounce of stay-fit motivation I can muster.

chapter•six

restoke your engine

Short of major surgery, I can't imagine anything that quite knocks the wind out of your sails like delivering a baby. Seriously. Even if you're lucky enough to make a quick recovery, childbirth totally and utterly kicks a gal's ass (and if you've had a C-section, you get the delightful double whammy of labor and delivery and major surgery—such fun).

On top of it all, your work is so not finished once the wee one is out and about. Somehow, you've got to find the energy to keep that little creature alive. And as you read on, you'll learn precisely how to do that, from beefing up the amount of omega vitamins in your diet to spacing out your meals and snacks so you're constantly fueled throughout the day. You'll also see the role adequate water consumption plays in staying peppy, and why all the quick fixes we naturally gravitate toward (read: endless cups of java) can actually produce the opposite effect than the one a new mama is after.

hello? you just built a whole new person

The ten fingers. The ten toes. The unspeakably adorable body that wiggles in-between those darling digits. The cherubic head that sits on top of it all, charming you to pieces with its gurgles, loving gazes, and gummy smiles. You made all that. Every last cell.

So is it any wonder your postpartum body is completely depleted after literally "donating" bits and pieces of yourself to the baby-making cause? Key vitamins, minerals, amino acids, fats, and enzymes have all gone into the creation of your DD. Let's take a few key essential fatty acids—omegas three, six, and nine—as just one example. According to Tanya Mackay, a cocreator of the cult-hit skincare line Mama Mio, the fetus snatches up your body's omegas, which are responsible for skin elasticity, a healthy immune system, and function of the brain, eye, and nervous systems, during pregnancy and lactation. And you want that to happen, by the way, because they assist in the growth of your baby's brain. But if your own stores of omegas were seriously depleted during pregnancy—and there's a high likelihood they were—you're at risk for a host of woes ranging from superficial bummers like stretch marks to major hormonal flux and baby blues. Since our bodies can't manufacture omegas on their own, they've got to come from somewhere, whether it's via fish oil supplements, green leafy vegetables, or other sources.

Two-time mama Mara has had great success adding omegas to her lengthy list of energizers. "I'm definitely a caffeine junkie, but trying to reform," she says, noting that she also tries to get enough sleep, exercise, and water to keep her batteries charged. "And I'm eating lots of omegas. I find that when I include them in the form of flaxseed on oatmeal, walnuts on a salad, or eating salmon for dinner, I just feel better. I can be distracted during the day by any number of things—a new Facebook friend, preschool registration—so I need all the help I can get in the staying-focused department," Mara adds. "Omegas are doing that for me."

Of course, while hugely important, omegas are just one piece of the nutritional puzzle impacted by pregnancy. And while you were probably advised by your ob-gyn to keep taking your prenatal vitamins postdelivery, that isn't a long-term strategy. Why not? Because your pregnancy nutrient needs vary drastically from your postpartum needs. This is especially true if you lost a lot of blood in the delivery process, either through C-section, or, as with me, cesarean plus postpartum hemorrhage.

At the risk of repeating myself, I'd highly recommend a visit to a good nutritionist or holistic practitioner to put you back on the path to wellness, particularly if you're feeling flat-out exhausted. "I went to see my Chinese doctor to talk about low energy and she gave me a couple of herbal tonics to try," says twins mama Christine. "They taste awful but they seem to help. She calls them 'blood builders.' I think she's trying to replenish my body with all of the little things gestating two human beings took away!" Also, as I noted in Chapter 4, a simple blood test can pinpoint exactly which nutrients have gone AWOL during gestation. You'll want to rule out anemia and thyroid problems; although they're usually short-lived, postpartum thyroid issues are not uncommon and can be a big cause of fatigue.

Keep in mind that knowledge is power, and the faster you know what you're up against the faster you can catch the bus back to Perkyville. If a trip to the doc isn't viable at the moment, at least make a major effort to eat a wide variety of nutrient-rich foods. One easy way to make sure you're doing that is to strive for a "rainbow" of fruits and vegetables in your diet. The more intense the color—think arugula rather than iceberg lettuce—the better for your body. Oh, and be sure to check out the books I recommend in the Dig Deeper Appendix!

sleep is only part of the equation

Sleep is crazy-important, so much so that I've devoted the entirety of Chapter 18 to snoozing. But of the three big energizers—sleep, sound nutrition, and exercise—guess which one you have the least control over in the first few months after delivery? Bingo—sleep! Even if you have help, there's a very good chance you're breastfeeding, which makes deep, restful, uninterrupted sleep a near impossibility.

reserve the right to . . .

. . . give into couch cravings on occasion. As long as you're taking good care of yourself, there's nothing wrong with declaring a movement embargo from time to time. I find it helpful just to say it out loud: "Tonight, I am officially a chore-free zone." And with remote in hand, I plop right down and click on the Tivo.

We've touched on food here, and we'll be diving into it big time in Chapter 7, but it's important to realize that it's not just what you eat, it's how you eat that affects your energy levels. Lots of food gurus are proponents of mini meals, which spread the nutritional fuel over an entire day rather than breaking it up into three biggish feasts. The idea is that you never let yourself get so hungry or so full that your blood sugar levels peak and valley all over the place, taking your mood and energy stores along with them.

Exercise is the ultimate Catch-22 of the energy picture. You're too tired to work out, but if you could just make yourself do it you'd have more get up and go. Although I'm completely blissed out to report that I've been sleeping really well lately, just last night I woke up at 2:00 A.M. ruminating over a whole lot of useless nonsense. Despite lying awake for hours, I forced myself to jump rope this morning rather than just going through the shower/dress/head-to-work routine. And guess what? I've buzzed through this entire day with enough oomph to get everything done that I needed to do. Love that!

So how does working out fire you up for other activities? "Exercise improves your metabolism, thereby giving you more energy," says *Lose That Baby Fat!* author Chabut. "Moving your body with gentle exercise also speeds up your circulation and helps get the blood flowing, which increases your energy level. And it boosts your mood by releasing endorphins, reducing stress, and improving your sense of well-being."

On those days when you'd rather insert toothpicks into your eyeballs than exercise, I suggest tricking yourself. Say, "I'll just do ten minutes, and then if I feel like quitting, I'll bail and watch *Judge Judy.*" I can almost guarantee that once the oxygen starts flowing, those ten minutes will turn into twenty or maybe even thirty. And if they don't, well at least you got ten minutes in. Woo-hoo!

h2omg: if i see one more water bottle . . .

A whopper of a sleep deficit is of course one big reason why you feel like crawling under the nearest rock, but there's also an excellent chance that you're dehydrated. And here's something else I learned while researching this book: Not only can dehydration masquerade as fatigue, it can also disguise itself as hunger. So, on those days when you're even more tired than usual or hungry enough to eat virtually everything in sight, it could very well be that you haven't consumed enough agua.

And there's even one more dastardly thing we can pin on not having enough water circulating throughout our bods: "mommy brain." I'm sure you're familiar with this condition, which manifests in the inability to remember your baby's name from time to time or the misplacement of your house keys ten times in the space of fifteen minutes. The precise action by which water energizes the brain, and in turn energizes the body, is fairly complex, but I'll try to sum it up as succinctly as I can.

Dehydration triggers a reduction in blood flow, which slows down the brain. Additionally, when water flows freely between cells, it delivers nutrients to their proper places, spirits away toxins, and generates a specific type of energy that the brain thrives on. A frisky brain means a frisky body, but here's what's kooky: You can just be laying there like a massive couch potato and still lose water. According to the Mayo Clinic, the average person, even without exercising, loses ten cups of fluids per day.

Now consider what you as a mom to a demanding newborn go through each day, especially if you're breastfeeding. You're probably on the go from the second you wake up in the morning until you hit the sheets many, many hours later. So it only makes sense that your water needs are ratcheted way up.

So what's the optimal amount? There's been a lot of debate about this lately, as well as a debunking of the "eight glasses a day" guideline. Personally, I try to drink at least one liter a day, and that's just at the office. Between morning and evening sipping, I'm probably tacking on another half liter.

Know that it's important to keep drinking regardless of whether you feel genuine thirst, because by the time you feel thirsty you may already be depleted. There are a few easy ways to tell if you need more water: If you're constantly reaching for lip balm to quench your parched pucker or if your pee isn't clear in color you're probably dehydrated.

energy zappers: caffeine, sugar, booze

When you're feeling wiped out (a natural state for any new mama), it makes perfect sense to reach for whatever you feel will give you an instant lift. Just don't get sucked in by false energizers like a massive cup of joe or a pound of chocolate. Because while those might provide a little jolt, they aren't without side effects. And as for that nightly glass of vino you've grown to love after you tuck your tot in? There's a good chance it's disrupting your slumber, and there's nothing remotely energizing about a sleep deficit.

Caffeine

How do I write this section without sounding like the biggest hypocrite on the planet? Me, who positively lives for her morning coffee? I'll admit that I have a love-hate thing going on with java. Over the years, I've tried to "kick" my habit several times, and I have, for weeks on end. In fact, I even lasted a couple of months once. With the exception of the first trimester of my pregnancy, in which I steered clear for fear of miscarriage, all of those cold-turkey no-coffee stints were prompted by my decades-long intermittent anxiety. And to this day, if I'm in crisis mode and not sleeping, coffee is the first thing that gets the heave-ho.

During my last sleepless stretch, I became quite smitten with what I call "foffee"—fake coffee from this company called Teeccino that my assistant turned me on to. I have to say it was pretty delish, and really helped me through that rough patch until I inevitably fell off the wagon and starting drinking the real stuff again.

If you ever want to learn about the evils of caffeine, trot on over to the Teeccino website (*www.teeccino.com*). There you'll learn that the addictive aromatic liquid has been linked to all manner of health woes, including irritable bowl syndrome, migraines, and an elevation of cortisol, the body's main stress hormone. But here's what really scares me: it might be making me fat. That's because it raises insulin levels, which causes a corresponding drop in blood sugar and subsequent craving for high-fat, high-carb fare.

If you're convinced you need caffeine—and I'm sure most new mamas feel it's necessary, at least in the early postpartum period—try getting it from a healthier source. Kirsch cites green tea, which delivers almost as much caffeine as coffee, as one of his favorite pick-me-ups. "It has polyphenols," he says, referring to a particular type of antioxidant that helps stem oxidative stress, the source of much chronic disease. "It's very healthy and it's a great source of energy." FYI, there was a study that came out a few years ago linking green tea to liver damage, but that's at extremely high doses—levels that can only be obtained through supplements. If you're just sipping the stuff, you can actually work your way through ten small cups a day without major risk to your liver.

the**mother**load

"I try to eat better to boost my energy, but I think I'll just be tired until they're 18 years old! I never feel that I can catch up completely, and have as much energy as I used to. But I take more vitamins now than I had before."

—**Jenny R.**, mama of twins

Some of Kirsch's other favorite energizers include "vitamin B12 in supplement form, beans, and healthy carbs." And when you just need to grab something quick, he's a big fan of almonds, walnuts, and apples. "Those are all great power-energy foods," he says.

Sugar

If there's one kind of pseudofood that really wreaks havoc on your get up and go, it's sugar. No matter what form it's in (pure cane or any of the "-oses"—sucrose, dextrose, maltose)—sugar sets up a particularly vicious cycle. After you imbibe, you get a short-lived rush, followed by a crash, and then a craving for more. (Hmmm . . . sounds a little like another powdery white substance, but that one's illegal.)

I have sugar "issues," for sure. I'm the type of person who absolutely, categorically should not have sugary treats in the house because I can't be trusted to "just have one." One doesn't cut it for me, and since I have a husband who insists on having something yummy in the freezer or pantry at all times, I'm basically screwed. It takes a lot of willpower to steer clear of Hubby's goodies, like the gourmet chocolate chip cookies he routinely stashes in his home-office filing cabinet. But since I believe in taking responsibility for myself and not playing the blame game, I just suck it up by keeping lots of delicious organic fruit around. Knowing that eating sugar is messing with my energy levels and packing inches on my thighs is a powerful incentive to not start eating it in the first place.

Booze

Unlike caffeine or the white stuff, no one reaches for a glass of wine for energy. Rather, relaxation and stress relief are key reasons women cite for hitting the vino after a long day of watching the baby. And guess what? It can really help on that front. But if you're in the habit of pounding a glass or two of wine as a sleep aid, chances are it's backfiring on you by destroying your REM sleep. That's because it creates mini withdrawal symptoms once it starts to wear off, causing an abbreviated first REM cycle followed by fitful subsequent cycles. So sure, you might konk out fairly easily after that second Merlot, but you're also probably waking up many more times during the middle of the night than you would have had you sipped seltzer instead. Sorry to be a big buzz kill, but if you're tossing and turning when you really need to be snoozing and snoring, cool it with the wine coolers.

I know it won't be easy, but putting down the java, the bonbons, and the wine—or at least scaling way back—will result in long-term, lasting energy. And the self-discipline you'll be gaining will prove mighty helpful for the next chapter, in which we basically undo any bad dietary habits you may have latched onto during your eat-anything-that-isn't-nailed-down preggo phase.

worked for me!

Balancing My pH Level

As a longtime beauty editor, I've sat through many a weird and wacky new-product presentation. Once they start trotting out the charts and diagrams of the latest, greatest wrinkle-busting nanotechnology, I'm mentally halfway out the door.

But every once in a while, my ears perk up and I open my mind to the possibility that maybe, just maybe, something might actually work. Such was the case at the launch event for the book *Stop Aging, Start Living: The Revolutionary Two-Week pH Diet That Erases Wrinkles, Beautifies Skin, And Makes You Feel Fantastic* by dermatologist Jeanette Graf. The doc, a bundle of energy with piercing blue eyes, is a proponent of balancing your pH level and is convinced it's the secret to not only stopping the clock, but also to feeling great and warding off serious illness.

After my second skin-cancer scare, I cracked open Dr. Graf's book and started reading. Sadly, right off the bat, I learned that two of my favorite bevvies—diet cola and coffee—boost your acidity, which is not good. Rather, you want to tip the scales in the opposite, or alkaline, direction. Other acidifiers include sugar, processed carbs, alcohol, and animal protein from meat and dairy, all the stuff I already feel guilty about consuming. By swapping in lots of fruits and veggies, filtered water, leafy greens, and nuts to replace the "baddies," you'll be on your way to a more balanced, healthier body. For me, one of the easiest tweaks was to have a hot cup of lemon water first thing in the morning. (It sounds counter intuitive, but citrus is alkalinizing rather than acid producing. Go figure.) I also nabbed some handy drops, called Health Resources Alkaline Body Balance (*www.healthresources.net*), from my local health food store and just squirt them into water or whatever else I'm drinking.

Although there's tons of research in Dr. Graf's book, I won't even begin to try to distill it for you. But I will say that the weeks I've really tried to stick to the balanced pH plan, I've pHelt absolutely terrific.

step away from the cupcake: "eating for two" is officially over

From stretch marks to spider veins, that little freeloader in the crib in the next room can be blamed for a long list of postpartum health and beauty woes. But those thirty extra pounds welded to your midsection ten months after delivery? Not so much.

Though I'm a complete math moron, let me just run some numbers for you: You were probably advised by your ob-gyn to keep your total pregnancy weight gain under thirty-five pounds. Once you subtract an average of six to ten pounds of baby, up to two pounds of placenta, and another two to three pounds of amniotic fluid, it's up to you to shed that last twenty. And if you have much more than that hanging around, it's probably because you went a little bonkers with the Cinnabons.

Look, I get it. You couldn't have sushi or booze for forty weeks, so in retaliation you decided to polish off a pint or five of ice cream or some other gazillion-calorie treat every night. And all that indulging would be perfectly cool if weren't so gosh-darn "challenging" to stop doing it once the DD arrives. But ask yourself this: Why, when life is exponentially harder (i.e., in those first few zombie-ish postpartum weeks and months), would we have some sudden explosion of willpower? In other words, if it's 3:00 A.M. and you're staring down a bag (or box or pint) of your favorite goody while your newborn is busy nuzzling away at your boobs—or worse, screaming her precious little head off—it would be next to impossible to resist. Obviously, those aren't the best conditions for getting back on track foodwise. But if you make the commitment—and that's what it takes, a full-on pledge to yourself to start becoming more aware of the useless excess calories you consume—you'll get there. One rejected donut at a time.

first, cut yourself some slack . . .

Although many a stupid joke has been cracked about preggos sending some poor loved one out in the middle of a blizzard for chocolate-covered jalapeño peppers or some other wacky concoction, cravings for specific foods are real. Not every pregnant woman gets them, but plenty do. And sometimes, rather than lusting after some obscure, off-the-grid treat, expectant mamas are just plain starving. But while preggos often naturally crave more calories, that isn't a free pass to just eat anything. In other words, not all cravings are considered equal, nutritionally speaking.

According to Dr. Jeffrey Morrison, whom you "met" in Chapter 4, hormones—yes, those hideous entities again—are the chief culprits behind the desire to dive into the nearest vat of Rocky Road or dill pickles. While he doesn't clap his hands with glee when his pregnant patients eat a bunch of dodgy crapola, he finds some dietary additions worthwhile. "Cravings are very person-dependent," he says. "Pregnancy shouldn't be carte blanche to drink soda and eat fast food every night, but some women actually end up broadening their healthy food choices. Like vegetarians might start craving red meat or women on low-carb diets might want carbs. In balance, it's all okay." During my own pregnancy, I tried to ease up on my own vegetarianism by having steak occasionally. Whatever guilt I felt was offset by the knowledge that I was giving my unborn baby the extra doses of iron, protein, and vitamin B12 she (and probably I, too) needed.

. . . then, get a plan

Now that you're no longer anticipating your DD, the jig is up. You have to get a grip on the excessive noshing. The key to reining in out of control eating is to have a plan. If you're still on maternity leave or have decided to stop working to stay home with your baby, you'll actually need two plans. The first is to structure your day so that eating doesn't become what nutrition guru and *Body After Baby* author Jackie Keller describes as a "default activity"—that thing we do almost unconsciously when we're bored out of our minds. When it's just you, the baby, and the four walls to contend with for eight or nine hours until Hubby walks in the door, boredom is all but guaranteed. Factor in kitchen proximity and you just might find yourself fighting quite a battle of the bulge.

The second plan that every postpartum mama needs, regardless of whether she's heading back to work or not, is to start substituting healthy, lower-calorie fare for all the crummy stuff. Think of it as swapping the good guys for the bad guys.

If you do this slowly, in baby steps, it won't feel like you've just lost your strawberry-frosted BFF, and within time, the garbage will lose its power. Even sugar doesn't need to hold you in its creepy little clenches. Though I've personally found that the more sugar I eat the more I want to eat, not everyone is a slave to the white stuff. "For some women, just a little bit of something sweet takes away the feeling of deprivation," says Keller. "And there's a huge psychological benefit, for some, in having sweets. So I'm of the mind that you're better off incorporating a little bit into your daily meal plan."

The key to success with this "little bit" system is to really enjoy your snack du jour and relax in the knowledge that it's always going to be there for you. "That way," says Keller, "you don't feel like you need to eat the whole box of cookies or chocolates because you can always have more the next day," she explains. "I think giving yourself permission, within limits, is healthy. Telling yourself that this is the only time you can enjoy something—because then it's back to the semi-starvation regimen—is what sets you up for one of those 'eat the whole box' episodes."

reserve the right to . . .

. . . devour an entire pint of Chubby Hubby after a really bad day. Just make sure those "bad days" happen, at most, only once a month. Or better yet, keep a stash of popsicles on hand. They're a supersmart swap when you're craving something sweet and icy cold. I like Edy's Fruit Bars because they're low cal and naturally delicious.

There are myriad approaches to tackling the better-eating thing, not to mention umpteen diet books and weight-loss websites (I've listed some of my favorites in the Dig Deeper Appendix). In fact, there's so much info out there that sifting through it could easily be a full-time job. But I'm convinced that what it really boils down to is habits. Swapping out a banana and a handful of raisins for a Snickers bar has to become automatic.

Basically, becoming a more mindful eater, one who consistently makes good food choices and has full control over that 813-calorie Cinnabon Classic rather than vice versa, involves taking the following steps.

Educate Yourself

Despite the fact that I eat it on occasion, I'm not a big fan of processed, packaged, or fast food. That's why I love books like *Eat This, Not That,* that allow you to make informed choices, whether it's in the potato chip aisle at the supermarket or the drive-through at Taco Bell. Grab a copy (details in the Dig Deeper Appendix), look up your favorite sinful goodies, and find a healthier substitute. And with all the calorie labeling in fast-food joints and supermarkets these days, you can also make better grub decisions simply by opening your eyes. Yes, looking at labels is a big buzz kill, but at least you'll know where you stand, caloriewise.

Break It Down

If you're not up for overhauling your entire diet, tackle one meal at a time. Start with, say, a Breakfast Momover, and swap in a bowl of fresh fruit or plain lowfat yogurt sprinkled with cinnamon for the insanely fattening megamuffin you usually scarf. By the way, from a motivation standpoint, a healthy breakfast is crucial. If your first meal of the day is a towering stack of chocolate-chip pancakes topped with whipped cream, you're far more likely to throw in the towel and shovel in garbage the rest of the day.

Once you're successful with one piece of your day (e.g., breakfast), move on to the next. Before you know it, you'll get through an entire twenty-four hours without eating anything dodgy. Once you master one day, keep on trucking until if feels completely freaky and weird to eat badly. You'll have your bad days (hours, minutes, seconds), but they don't have to completely unravel your commitment. If you blow it, just dust yourself off and start over again.

keep a paper trail (or log on and lose it)

One way to keep yourself "honest" on the food front is to keep a food log. There's just something about knowing she'll have to jot down "one-half roll of peanut butter cookie dough" in a daily food log that makes a wannabe hot mama less inclined to eat it. No matter how much self-esteem you have (and hopefully it's plenty), that just isn't going to feel good. Conversely, "brown rice and veggies" looks positively smashing in print and instills a real sense of pride as it flows out of your pen and onto the page. "Egg-white omelet" and "baked halibut and sweet potatoes" are pretty cool to write down, too.

Look, I would never suggest for a moment that keeping a food journal is fun, but there's no question—absolutely none, nada, zip—that it's an effective tool in weight loss and better eating. So let me just tick off the reasons why you'll be more likely to lose blubber if you track what you're eating than if you just wing it and hope for the best: One, you won't conveniently "forget" all the little nibbles here and there that add up big time over the course of the day. Two, you'll see where your diet is deficient (e.g., too many carbs, not enough fruits, etc.). Three, you'll be able to look back on your "good" days and celebrate your self-discipline and all-around sterling moral character.

The trick is to find the method that's easiest for you. While I'm no gadget girl, I'm sort of loving the online food trackers. Although some, like the excellent "My Food Diary" (*www.myfooddiary.com*) charge a small monthly fee, it might be one of the best investments you'll ever make in yourself. Not only will you be able to list your food intake, you can also search a database of common foods and determine calories, fats, carbs, etc. In addition, you can record your exercise for the day. So it's pretty much like one-stop shopping for a fitter, healthier bod. Got to love that!

just don't go overboard, especially if you're breastfeeding

Obviously, I think most new mothers, myself included, need to be a little harder on ourselves when it comes to eating better. That's because there are probably a good twenty times each day when you're faced with making the choice between a food that's healthy (read: nourishing, vitamin packed, and low in calories) and one that doesn't have much going for it other than taste and the seemingly miraculous ability to latch onto your ass and stay there for a few years, and trust me when I tell you that I make bad choices all the time.

the**mother**load

"I could pretty much wolf down whatever I wanted prekids and while I was breastfeeding, but now I find I pack on the pounds when I overindulge. So I've started cooking a little lighter and I try not to buy cookies or sweet treats. Instead, I stick to dark chocolate and fruit yogurt."

—**Ninka**, mama of two

Despite nudging you to become much more aware and mindful of what you're eating, I don't want you to become completely obsessed and start eliminating entire food groups. That's especially true if you're breastfeeding. Contrary to all the old wives' tales, there are very few foods that, when eaten by Mama, actually have a negative effect on Baby.

Keller admits to complete frustration when new-mom clients of hers buy into the misinformation surrounding some of the healthiest foods out there, namely dairy products, beans, and cruciferous vegetables such as broccoli, cabbage, and kale. Although some of these foods can indeed make you gassy, any residual gassiness passed along to your baby will be minimal and short lived. "I find that there are many more neuroses around eating well when you're breastfeeding than there are around eating well when you're pregnant," she says. "And there are a lot of conflicting opinions among ob-gyns, doulas, nannies, lactation experts—you name it—so women are much more confused about what to eat while they're nursing. There's a tremendous emphasis on eliminating certain whole categories of foods because there's some belief that they'll make your baby uncomfortable. But that compromises your immune system, because a lot of the best immunity-boosting, antioxidant-rich foods are in the cruciferous family."

If you're absolutely convinced there's a real problem—for example, if you think your tot is allergic to dairy—discuss the matter with your pediatrician. Then, you can remove all dairy products from your diet for two weeks and gradually reintroduce them, one at a time, to sleuth out the prime suspects. But while you're doing that, make sure you're getting adequate calcium either via other foods or a supplement prescribed for you by your doctor.

For those of you who don't have any fussy-baby issues, make it your business to eat sensibly, picking from a wide assortment of foods so you can get as many vitamins and nutrients as possible. Just do your best and get on with your incredibly busy life. After all, you have zero time to waste, especially since you'll be raising your game on the fitness front momentarily. You'll be making some big decisions, too, about whether to work out with or without le bébé. And away we go!

worked for me!

Mail-Order Mangoes

Recently, after twenty-five amazing years living like a caged animal in Manhattan, Hubby had the audacity to pry me out. He dragged me kicking and screaming across the Hudson River to Jersey City, which is maybe a whole mile, as the crow flies, away from our former New York digs. Still, for the first few months, our new neighborhood felt like Guam.

Now that we're settled in, however, and I'm holding meditation sessions in my massive walk-in closet, I'm utterly smitten with "country living." There's just one teensy problem: The brand-new supermarket downstairs in our condominium complex, which is easily twenty times larger than the tiny rat trap we used to shop in, has an inexplicably microscopic organic produce section. I don't get it; there are plenty of nonorganic fruits and veggies, mind you—row after pristine row—but good luck finding a halfway decent peach or pear that hasn't been sprayed to smithereens with pesticides.

Since keeping mouth-watering fruit on hand at all times is a key way I try to keep the chocolate-cookie binges at bay, I've taken matters into my own hands via the U.S. mail. Specifically, Harry & David's Organic Fruit of the Month Club *(www.harryanddavid.com)*. Every thirty days, a box arrives filled with the world's most perfect-looking organic something-or-other, be it crisp Fuji apples, navel oranges, honey mangoes, or golden pineapples. Yum. (Don't freak, you don't have to commit to an entire year if you're not up for that.)

When I get desperate, I'll grab a nonorganic piece of fruit here and there because, let's face it, even a nonorganic banana or handful of berries beats the nutritional hell out of a Krispy Kreme. And even if I don't have my precious favorite produce wash on hand (Environné, nab some at *www.vegiwash.com*) to rinse off the beastly pesticides, I just go for it. Then I go home and check the mail.

chapter•eight

exercise: to baby or not to baby

Confession time: Because I can't even fathom wanting to work out with my DD anywhere near me, this chapter was among the most challenging for me to write. But before anyone sics the Mommy Police on me, please know that I'm actually a nice person. I'd even venture to say I'm a primo mama. It's just that I'm so fond of monotasking that the idea of tossing the tot into the exercise mix makes me feel all off center and distracted.

That's why I love what I do for a living. Now that I've slipped on my reporter's cap, dug into my research, chatted with experts, and explored the issue from different angles, I can definitely see why some mothers swear by their favorite Mommy and Me classes. And from a health perspective, if it boils down to making the choice between working out with your DD or not at all, by all means, strap that sweetie in the baby carrier pronto. The important thing is to get moving, in whatever manner "speaks" to you. If you're on the fence about whether to include the tot or not, read on.

strength in numbers

Within the past decade, the market for mommy-and-me-style fitness classes has grown by leaps and bounds. Just look at the success of Stroller Strides alone; as I write this, there are now more than 300 franchises dotting cities and suburbs across the country. (To locate a class near you, visit *www.strollerstrides.com*.) Once you add in other types of stroller workouts (Stroller Fit, Strollercise, Baby Boot Camp, etc.) and the multitude of mommy-baby yoga classes, it's pretty clear that thousands of fitness-minded women don't share my aversion to exercising with a tiny tot in tow. One need only scan the testimonials on the websites for some of these exercise programs to know that lots of new mamas are happily losing inches and building friendships as they hit the hiking trail or yoga mat with their little darlings plopped on top of their tummies.

the**mother**load

"I loved having my Pilates instructor come to my home to train me. It was perfect. I can remember doing exercises on the Reformer machine with my baby sitting on my belly. I tried to schedule the sessions for when he was napping, but that didn't always work out."

—Katherine, mama of one

Obviously, there are two schools of thought on this topic. So after doing some reconnaissance work, here's what I see as the pros and cons of working out *avec bébé*.

Benefits of mommy-baby classes:

- Allow you to just be your chubby postbaby self; no competing with the spandex-clad hotties at your regular gym
- Provide regular adult interaction—highly desirable if you're on maternity leave
- Save on the sitter costs you'd fork over if you headed to yoga all by your lonesome
- Get you out of the house (and away from the refrigerator, freezer, and pantry)
- Provide a little fresh air and a chance to commune with nature (if they're held outdoors)
- Set a good fitness example for the tot from a very young age
- Zap any (misplaced) guilt about taking time for yourself to exercise

Drawbacks of mommy-baby classes:

- Are not as flexible, schedulewise, as working out at home; you have to be somewhere at a designated time
- Loading up the car with diaper bags, snacks, and strollers for the to-and-fro trips is a much bigger pain than pushing the coffee table aside for some quick ab work
- Attention is divided between following the instructor and caring for the baby
- Excessive socializing with the other mamas can result in a half-assed workout

Not that you need to actually go someplace to exercise with your baby. Amazon is positively teeming with workout DVDs that can be done as a duet. There are books, too, although I can only imagine how tricky it would be to simultaneously flip through one of those, keep the DD where you want her, and execute the required moves in some type of semismooth, purposeful fashion. Still, for those who feel they learn best clutching a book in their hands, I've included a few recommendations in the Dig Deeper Appendix. And even if you find a few books or DVDs that you really like, you can always switch up your workouts with some outdoor action. Just strap your lad or lassie into a sturdy carrier or stroller and get going.

less talking, more walking

Perhaps you're the outgoing type, someone who, prebaby, loved nothing more than the camaraderie of your regular Thursday night Bikram yoga class. Or maybe you're such a "people person" that you genuinely liked working out in a sea of treadmills and elliptical machines at one of those open-all-hours megagyms. If you've nodded your head at any of those descriptions, a mommy-baby class is probably a good bet for you.

Depending on where you are on the postpartum scale, your energy levels and fitness requirements are bound to vary. If you're just past the doctor-approved six-week mark, you're surely not ready—at least physically—for any major activity. Because of the not-quite-yourself-yet state you're in, it might be a great time to check out a gentle, low-key mommy-baby postnatal yoga or Pilates class. Just don't expect to walk out with a six-pack. If you're a complete newbie, simply mastering the moves will seem like a massive accomplishment. But even if you're a seasoned pro, between keeping your eye on the baby and your postpartum energy deficit in those early weeks and months, you might not get anywhere near the workout you're used to.

You can also check out the stroller programs, which, though I've never participated in one, seem a little more intense, at least from an aerobic standpoint. When you're not on the move strolling, you're being put through your paces with wall sits, leg lifts, crunches, etc. Of course, mucho chatting can thwart your intention to get a good workout. Not so much so in yoga and Pilates, because those disciplines are largely practiced in near silence. But when you're part of a big caravan of strollers, it's easy to lag behind with your bestie, and start gossiping and solving the world's problems with a little girl talk.

No matter what type of class or program you choose, there's an easy way to ensure you're making the whole venture worth your while: focus. In other words, dial into my personal mantra and do what you're doing. Sure, you might need to hop off to the sidelines to change a nappy or proffer a few minutes of boob to a hungry tot, but try to stay in the mental game during your mini time-out. Heck, you can even do a couple of squats or lunges while tending to baby if you feel so inclined. Just keep the chatting to a minimum, perhaps by making a phone date to catch up later that night when the babies are asleep.

raising your game: finding a tougher workout

In the initial postpartum period, when you need to take it easy anyway, your baby's relatively light bodyweight is ideal; a ten-pound kid is a heck of a lot easier to maneuver than one who clocks in at twenty or twenty-five. Then, just as exercising with your DD becomes unwieldy, your strength is, hopefully, also starting to bounce back. You might not be where you were prepregnancy, but you're on your way. Even so, I wouldn't recommend ditching postpartum classes altogether just yet. It's important to err on the safe side, guided by an instructor who knows the nuances of the new-mama body.

If you feel that you've outgrown your current class, in some cases, as with Baby Boot Camp, you can get a tougher workout within the same program. This could mean moving from sixty to seventy-five minutes or shifting to the next level of class, which will probably entail both more cardio and additional strengthening exercises.

If you feel you've outgrown your first mommy-baby class and there aren't any higher levels within the program for you to aspire to, you may need to poke around for another scenario with a slightly more rigorous approach. Not that you have lots of free time on your hands (or virtually any, for that matter), but it pays to shop around. Most studios and gyms will let you sample a class or two à la carte before signing up for an entire package or membership, so be sure to try before you buy.

reserve the right to . . .

. . . semi-insist that your hubby or partner work out with you. Exercising *a deux* is a win-win for everyone: You'll be sneaking in some much-needed couple time and reducing bottled-up baby stress while you're at it. Even a long walk will get the blood flowing, especially if you're pumping your arms rather than pushing a stroller.

When she was creating the postnatal Pilates curriculum at her eponymous New York studio, owner Erika Bloom says the intention was to incorporate equal parts safety, fun for both mother and baby, and a solid core workout. "The truth is," Bloom recalls, "that moms really want to spend quality time with their kids. And the class benefits the children as well because they're rolling, adjusting to the movements, they're working on neck strength, interacting with their moms and other children, and they're getting stimulated. All of the exercises are geared to the mom getting stronger and the child getting stronger—and to interacting."

Still, it's not a total mosh pit. One reason Bloom's postnatal class is such a hit is because it's limited to just a handful of mommy-baby pairs. That way, everyone gets a good dose of targeted teacher time. "The classes are really fun," she says, "but they're all about safe core exercises."

it's okay to do your own thing

Even if you were a fan of the mommy-baby setup in the early post-partum period, you may reach a point when you want to shift gears and return to working out on your own. Six months seems to be a turning point for some new mothers, perhaps because that often dovetails with the rules and regulations for nurseries at most athletic clubs. Though it's becoming increasingly common for gyms to have nurseries (a massive boon for fitness-minded moms), most won't let you drop your tot off with the staff babysitter until he or she is at least six months old.

If working out with your DD never held any appeal, don't feel bad. You're already doing plenty of activities together, and will be doing millions more in the years to come. Reserving an area of your life just for yourself, especially one that has such important health ramifications and deserves to be taken seriously, is not only allowed, it's a really great idea. Just be sure to devise some way of keeping yourself on track. Though it's easy to give way to chatting in a mommy-baby class, some mothers say they're convinced they work out harder in a group setting than they ever would at home on their own. It's true that it takes a sizeable amount of self-direction to stick to an exercise routine when no one is around to prod you along.

For example, I usually try to get my workout out of the way first thing in the morning, but from time to time, I decide to do a little writing first instead. However, this can backfire on me motivation-wise, as when I instead find umpteen million other things to do after writing except exercise. At these times, it takes a major amount of effort to will myself onto that mini trampoline or elliptical or to grab the jump rope. Since I know how important it is to stick to a routine, I just flat-out force myself. Then I make a mental note to remember that working out before the day officially starts is the best course of action for me.

Still, especially while your baby is really young, it's important to stay flexible about your fitness routine and just roll with the proverbial punches, says Chabut. "When your baby is a newborn, all they do is sleep," she notes. "It's easier to fit in a workout or go stroller walking while the baby is young and napping—you know they all fall asleep the moment you take them outside! However, as the baby gets older, carving out time for yourself and enlisting the help of a friend or a relative or even taking advantage of the childcare available at your local gym helps you focus more. The perfect scenario would be to get in some workouts by yourself and combine them with a mommy-and-me workout once a week so you can bond with your baby."

Even if you don't have oodles of time at your disposal (and really, what new mother does?), exercise should still be a big priority for you, especially if you still have a sizeable chunk of baby weight to shed. Besides, as you'll learn in the next chapter, there are lots of ways to squeeze in a workout. So move it, Mama!

worked for me!

Flying Solo

I shudder to think of how many great friends I may have made in a mommy-and-me type of exercise class (not to mention the pounds and inches I might have lost), but I've never been one for group fitness. That's partly because I'm pretty spazzy, and have always had a tough time keeping up with any kind of routine involving a series of sequential moves. But mostly it's because I like to work out when the mood strikes, not at a specific hour at a specific spot.

So after I blasted through a few ten packs of sessions with my fantabulous personal trainer during my early postpartum phase, I decided to go it totally alone again, and I've done that ever since. But now I've really got my work cut out for me; given my age and the havoc wreaked on my body by my DD, there's a lot to be done, including tightening my still-flabby belly.

If I didn't have a sizeable amount of self-discipline, I'd be a goner, but there's room for improvement on that front, too. After all, there's always some excuse not to exercise, especially with an adorable toddler tugging at your skirt hem, beseeching you to watch *Dora the Explorer* with her. To stay on track, I rely heavily on my little fitness log. I know I keep yammering about it, but it's just because I find it so damn helpful. I get energized looking back and seeing that on Monday, I cranked through 2024 jumps with the rope (relax, it has a built-in counter—I'm way too brain dead in the morning to count to 2000). A few days later, I powered through a thirty-minute jog on the treadmill, followed by a session on the elliptical the day after that.

Listen, I know some beat up little notebook isn't a substitute for a relationship I might have formed in the local chapter of Baby Boot Camp, but, to me, it sometimes seems like a very good friend indeed.

chapter•nine

the fast and the furious

For any gal who has ever counted the milliseconds until she could hop off the treadmill or elliptical (that would be me) or bitched and moaned her way through a session with a personal trainer (me again) or blew off working out for the flimsiest of reasons (you guessed it—moi), it can seem very ironic to start feeling deprived because you can't hit the gym on a regular basis. But that's exactly what happens when a baby knocks your once-orderly life on its once-shapely behind. Though it may be among the strangest sensations you'll ever experience, after several weeks of intensive baby care, you'll be dying to work up a sweat that isn't a byproduct of labor pains. Don't believe me? Well, I'm not the only one to experience this seemingly strange phenom.

"It's funny, but I used to think that thirty or forty-five minutes on a treadmill was just an eternity," says twins mama Christine. "I would just slog away at it, praying for the clock to move faster. Oddly enough, I'm much more patient at the gym than I used to be and I can't really explain it. And now, whenever I have the luxury of that much time, it goes by so fast! Even if I can only squeeze in a fifteen- or twenty-minute run or elliptical session, it's better than nothing at all. It's worth the trip even if I only have a half-hour to spare."

Guess what? It totally is. In fact, there's mounting evidence that, provided you really buckle down and work to raise your heart rate to its optimal level, quickie workouts broken out over the course of a day are every bit as valuable as one long megasession. So yes, from a physical standpoint, there's a compelling argument to just dive in and do a quickie workout, but I think the psychological benefits are just as important. For starters, even short sessions will help you feel like you're still "in the game" healthwise, which will have a positive spill-over effect on your food consumption (ever notice how motivating a five-pound weight loss is? You just want to keep up the good work rather than "reward" yourself with some 10,000-calorie hot fudge sundae). You're taking charge of your new postbaby life and showing the kind of flexibility that is the key to happy mothering. Once you're past the superdemanding newborn phase, all those brief, targeted workouts will make you stronger and more energized so you'll be able to blast out a long run or hour-long spinning class in no time flat.

focus, focus, focus

Now that I've trained myself to "do what I'm doing," I apply that credo to every area of my life, and I've found it to be especially helpful for staying fit. Real focus helps in so many ways, from honing in on a specific body part (which we'll get to in a bit) to getting in the right frame of mind. Ideally, switching out of "mom mode" into "fitness head" should be quick and painless.

Of course, with all you have on your plate right now, shifting mental gears can be challenging. In her no-nonsense book *15 Minute Everyday Pilates*, fitness author Alycea Ungaro, owner of Real Pilates NYC, notes that we often spend so much time mentally "getting ready" to exercise that we usually don't actually get around to doing it. Her advice: Try not to kick up a fuss before working out. Instead, save that energy for the exercise itself. As I've mentioned, I try to short circuit my own tendency to get distracted and procrastinate by working out as early in the day as possible. Above all, remember what a privilege it is to take such good care of yourself.

"I think motivation is just about repackaging exercise for yourself," says Ungaro. "Exercise really needs to be a reward. Get rid of that word 'work' in 'workout'—it's a trap. Instead, working out needs to be this awesome thing you do, this little treat. You need to think, 'I'm going to do this great thing for my body: I'm going to take care of my legs today.' Or, 'I'm going to strengthen my back.' Just say whatever you need to say to yourself that doesn't make exercise sound like work. Your inner dialogue is key; it's all about how you 'market' exercise to yourself." So, whether you knock it out in the morning or sometime later in the day, learn to harness your attention, in a really positive way, for the project ahead: working out quickly and efficiently.

Solution for a Short Attention Span

In her rockin' book *Lose That Baby Fat!*, Chabut makes a major case for lasering in on a short, no-drama workout a few times a day. (There are about a gazillion ten-minute routines sprinkled throughout her book.) "Doing shorter ten-minute workouts is realistic and cumulative—meaning it all adds up," she writes. "It also helps boost your metabolism by getting your heart rate up twice a day to burn calories more efficiently. And the best thing it does is to *not* let you use the excuse that you don't have enough time, because everybody has ten minutes." I couldn't agree more.

Because she's such a fountain of new-mom exercise advice, and is herself a time-starved mama of two, I called Chabut to pick her brains a bit more about the benefits of quickie workouts. "It's important for new moms to pace themselves," she says. "When they try to do too much, they can suffer setbacks from going too fast instead of building strength and stamina after giving birth." To prevent this, Chabut has her postpartum clients follow a "listen to your body" approach. "That's the best guide to identifying the right time to pick up the pace and increase your workouts," she says.

Rome wasn't built in a day, nor will you return to your pre-baby body that quickly. That's why, until your wee one gets a little older and you have more time to devote to fitness, you might consider prioritizing your main get-in-shape goal, be it increasing your strength, cardio fitness, or shedding weight. While it might be hard to pick a lane, it will certainly be a lot less intimidating than tackling all three sides of the total-fitness triangle at once. Then, once you recover a good chunk of your prebaby health and energy, you can get more ambitious. So what to pick? I say, do what will give you an immediate case of "the happys." If you're bummed about extra pounds, make weight loss your primary goal. If you want to be able to hoist your tot and all that gear and not feel like your back is about to split in half, concentrate on strength training. You see where I'm going with all this: Get a little bang for your exertion buck, psychologically as well as physically.

home improvement: basic gear to have on hand

Besides a high-quality pair of shoes and an ultrasupportive sports bra to keep those tender postpartum knockers in place, there really isn't anything in the way of equipment standing between you and a decent workout.

Still, at least in the first few months, when you're likely to be slipping in ten minutes here and there in your house or neighborhood rather than blocking out bigger chunks of time to hop in the car to head to a gym, it would be nice to have a few pieces of equipment on hand to shake up your routine and challenge "bored" body parts. Consider the following the building blocks of a home mini gym:

- Nonstick mat for floor work
- Three sets of dumbbells (you can start as low as one, two, and three pounds)
- Fitness ball (purchased according to height for best fit)
- Resistance bands (available in light, medium, and heavy resistance; also purchased according to height)
- Jump rope (read about my personal favorite in "Worked for Me")
- Pedometer (for outdoor walks or treadmilling)
- Heart-rate monitor
- Fitness DVDs (I give a few recommendations in the Dig Deeper Appendix)

Later, if you have the space for them—and you're sure they'll actually get some use—you might consider adding an adjustable weight bench and/or a mini trampoline that can be used for both jogging in place and rebounding. A weight bench is great for doing pec exercises, like dumbbell flys, that lift sagging breasts. And, although it takes a little getting used to, rebounding (aka light jumping) on a mini trampoline delivers a long list of benefits. Not only is rebounding considered low impact and a more efficient calorie burner than jogging, it's believed to stimulate the lymphatic system, which in turn boosts immunity. In fairness, all forms of exercise give an indirect lift to your immune system because they reduce stress, and, depending on what type you're doing, can also strengthen the heart. But there's something about rebounding (and jumping rope, my all-time favorite exercise) that gets the lymph flowing and the toxins moving. (For more on lymph drainage via dry brushing the skin, see "Worked for Me" in Chapter 16.)

reserve the right to . . .

. . . declare the living room or den off limits when you're working out at home. To make it easier on the TV junkies in your household, pick up one of those dry-erase calendars the next time you're driving past a Staples or Office Depot. If your exercise time slots are clearly posted—and they're not smack dab in the middle of prime time——who could possibly give Mom a hard time?

divide and conquer: working one body part at a time

Since I love monotasking, I'm completely down with zeroing in on a single body part at a time. Actually, it's more like a body zone than a part. There's something so orderly about knowing that on Monday it's upper body, on Tuesday it's lower body, followed by a day of cardio. Of course, that's a dream scenario, right? There's no way in hell you'll be able to pull off a workout schedule like that with a baby living under the same roof, right? Wrong! I won't say it isn't challenging to work your way up to that kind of a stay-strong routine, but it is doable. That's the beauty of training a single zone at a time.

Happily, there are now tons of exercise DVDs that make the task of focusing on a particular body zone a snap. A lot of them suggest using light dumbbells, but you can and definitely should skip those until you've sufficiently recovered your predelivery strength.

Do avail yourself of any routine that allows you to tackle upper and lower body on separate days. Not only will you be thoroughly working out each zone far better than you would be if you merely blasted through a "circuit," your muscles get a chance to recover on their "off" days. Bonus points: Many of these routines are really fast, like ten minutes kind of fast.

feeling stronger every day

When I was sketching out the initial outline for this book, I envisioned that the section you're reading now would be all about weights. But I've lately come around to the notion that strength training is the better, broader goal for new moms. By definition, strength training encompasses the whole spectrum of exercises that simply use resistance to build muscle. You can do that with or without weights. So to that end, weight training is just a part of strength training. If and when you're ready to tackle weights, or get back to them if you've taken some time off after having the baby, go for it. The list of benefits to be gained is endless.

If weights are so good for you (and they truly are so good for you), why not just hit the rack and get lifting? A few reasons: One, relaxin, a hormone released during pregnancy, can cause your joints to be slightly loose, putting you at a temporarily increased risk for injury. Two, most women don't have a complete set of weights in their homes, so any serious training would necessitate a trip to the gym—not a plan most mothers of newborns can commit to. Three, if you're a total newbie, weights can be intimidating. I don't know about you, but in the first year after having my tot I just didn't feel up to nor had oodles of extra time for learning a whole new sport and physical discipline from scratch.

"I'm not vehemently opposed to weights for new moms," says Kirsch, "but I'm the 'no-excuses' guy. For a plan to work, a new mother needs to know that she can do it while she's in the nursery or when she's out strolling in the park. You don't need traditional equipment to just do a little mini boot camp."

So for now, the plan of attack should be to aim for overall, head-to-toe strengthening (say, through Pilates or multimuscle exercises like push-ups and squats) with maybe a few light dumbbell exercises to shore up the back and upper body—that crucial area, which, along with the core, gets pummeled by lugging the baby, stroller, and diaper bag around. Kirsch teaches a lot of moves that use the weight of his new-mom clients' own bodies to strengthen and tone. For instance, he loves old-school push-ups for lifting saggy boobs, planks for firming stretched-out abs, and lunges for whipping wayward tushes into shape. "New mothers need to be very careful about setting a course of action that's very doable, very attainable," he says. "It's easy to get discouraged, so it's important not to try for too much, too fast." So make like a tortoise rather than a hare, and don't add sky-high fitness goals to the list of stuff that might already be stressing you out. Be mindful and purposeful about working out and remember, always, that it all adds up.

quick blasts of cardio

By now, you're beginning to suss out the merits of short workouts, like busting out a few jumping jacks and squats. Quick, twenty-minute hits of steady-state cardio can also be beneficial, but only if you really hustle and exert yourself. Sorry to break the news to you, but if you're able to do anything besides watch a TV monitor while you're on a treadmill, stationary bike, or elliptical machine, you're not working hard enough to maximize your twenty minutes.

The easiest way—well not the easiest, but certainly the most efficient—way to increase your cardio fitness level is to use intervals, otherwise known as mixing up your usual, steady pace with mercifully short but still exhausting bursts of energy. This could mean jogging for five minutes then running much faster for two minutes then slowing down a bit, etc. Basically, it's just bouncing back and forth between "hard" and "slightly easier" for your entire workout session.

Another way to ensure you're really going for it is to use a heart-rate monitor. Most include a chest strap (for capturing the heart rate) and either a wristwatch-style or upper-arm device for displaying the info. Monitors range wildly in price—from under $50 to north of $500—depending on the amount of bells and whistles such as built-in stopwatches, workout memory, calorie-burn counters, etc. Because I like everything as basic as possible, I recently ordered a Mio Classic Select Petite, which doesn't have a chest strap, requires minimal programming, and is fashioned to fit mini wrists like mine. FYI, a great discount resource for all kinds of monitors, including Mio, is *www.heartratemonitorsusa.com*.

the**mother**load

"For now, I've come to terms with the limitations on my workouts. My goal is not to have the toned, svelte body of a twenty-five year old. My goal is to be healthy and maintain a good energy level for my husband, my children, and for myself. But my hope is that once my youngest is in school full time, I can work out more—and burn more calories—at the gym."

—Gwen, mama of two

Keep in mind that the idea behind interval training and monitoring your heart rate is to pack purpose into your workouts. If you're exercising for shorter amounts of time, it's important not to just wing it anymore. So, in addition to fussing around with your pace (slower, faster, much faster, slower again, etc.), try to rotate the machines you use. By mixing it up with the treadmill, elliptical, stationary bike, and maybe a rowing machine or an old-time stair climber, you'll target different sets of muscles.

If, unlike me, you're a person who likes classes, go for it. With one caveat: If you're not signing up for a class specifically geared to postnatal types, be sure you're really feeling up for it. Or just park yourself in the back of the room and exit stage left once you've had enough. Keep reminding yourself that every little bit helps, because it most definitely does. Today, you might last fifteen minutes in class, while next week it could be a whopping twenty-five. Who knows, before long you might even be devoting a healthy chunk of time just to streamlining your abs—the bane of many a new mama's existence. But don't dive into the deep end before you read all about the smartest, most effective way to tone your tummy, the subject of the next chapter. (Hint: It's not about crunches.)

Running and Jumping

Because I'm klutzy, exercise routines that require that I focus on more than, say, one move at a time, get me literally all tripped up. That's a big reason I love running and jumping rope. Since I'm sure you're dying to hear the other reasons, I won't keep you in suspense any longer.

With running, it's the mindfulness that keeps me coming back for more. I can easily slip into a little trance when I'm running. I guess it's like a moving meditation, in that I'm just living in the moment, tuning in to my breathing, my surroundings, and my feet striking the pavement. Other days, when I'm staring down a massive to-do list, running clears out the mental cobwebs and opens the floodgates to a lot of great ideas.

While it's more grueling, jumping rope delivers the same kind of rhythmic, turbo-charged aerobic benefit. It's hard work, but I make it easier on myself through my choice of equipment. For years, I've used a Tanita HealthyJump *(www.tanita.com)*, a rope that counts revolutions, so I don't even have to keep track of how many jumps I'm cranking out. There's a built-in calorie counter, too. Though I know I should care about that, most of the time I really don't.

When I'm running on a treadmill, I shoot for thirty minutes. Outdoors, it can be as few as twenty, depending on the route. With jumping rope, I aim for between 2,000 and 3,000 jumps, which would clock in at twenty to thirty minutes. Yes, a half-hour is a little longer than I've been yammering about in this chapter, so on days when I'm really crunched for time, I just pop in a Joyce Vedral DVD and blast through a quick fifteen-minute upper- or lower-body routine. No excuses, right? I have to practice what I preach.

chapter•ten

ab solution

E ven in my often-wacky career as a beauty and health journalist, it isn't every day that someone sticks a finger in my belly button at a press event. But in this case, the "someone" was stomach guru Julie Tupler, author of *Lose Your Mummy Tummy* and creator of the Tupler Technique, her very own approach to kicking those dreaded après-baby "muffin tops" to the curb.

So yes, I let Julie have her way with me, for reasons I'll reveal shortly. That's how desperate I am to finally, once and for all, get rid of my postpartum kangaroo pouch. I'm sure you'd like to do that, too; that's why I've snooped around to find the best ways to improve the look of your postbaby belly, from which stomach muscles to target (and how) to tummy-firming crèmes and a fairly extreme save-this-until-you're-damn-sure-you're-finished-having-babies surgical procedure.

stretched to your limits

Though slack stomach skin does naturally "rebound" a bit postbirth, for first-time mamas, it's simultaneously terrifying and fascinating to watch your belly explode over the course of forty weeks. Toward the end of the whole shebang, the skin is so taut you start to wonder why it just doesn't rip wide open. The good news, of course, is that it doesn't, but that's also the bad news. Because the skin gives and gives until there's barely any giving left, you've undoubtedly got a few rolls of extra "you" once your DD is out. That's just what happens with the birth of a singleton; imagine what mommies of multiples have to contend with!

Even more than drooping boobs (the subject of the next chapter), a beat-up belly is postbaby body-bummer numero uno. There's no more tangible reminder that you've given birth than a few handfuls of stomach that want to hang around. While I'm just now getting around to doing it myself—three years after delivering, mind you—I'm convinced there's a lot to be done to improve the function and look of my midsection. There are just too many flat-bellied hot mamas out there for me to believe otherwise.

Before we get into specifics about how you can tone, tighten, and camouflage slack skin, I think a little perspective is in order. For that, I'll hand the microphone over to Rebekah, a ripped, super-fit mother of two (she also happens to be a kick-ass hairstylist whose work is featured in numerous magazines, ad campaigns, and TV commercials). "I'm at the gym four times a week, schedule permitting, and I try to get to at least one yoga class a week to stretch everything out," Rebekah says. "I also stay away from man-made carbs. And even with all that, my stomach isn't what it was. The skin is still looser. But apart from surgery, it's as good as it can get. I think all moms should remember that when they look in the mirror or head to the gym." Got that?

core beliefs

As much as I'd love to pin the blame for my saggy midsection on my tot, the fact is that my stomach has never really been the kind you can bounce a quarter off. That's because I hate classic ab work. I simply despise it. I'd rather run five miles or jump rope for twenty minutes than do a single crunch.

So you can imagine my glee when, through the process of researching this chapter, I uncovered this bit of news from multiple reliable sources: Old-school stomach exercises like crunches are useless for reining in a postpartum belly. Not only that, they can actually make the situation worse! Of course, if you've been crunching away like a madwoman, you're probably not psyched to read this, but at least you'll know why your stomach isn't deflating the way you'd hoped, dreamed, and prayed it would.

Apparently the reason crunches—as well as other movements that sort of jut your gut forward, such as "bicycles" (aka crossovers that involve touching your elbow to the opposite knee) and the Pilates 100, which entails jackknifing while pumping your arms— don't help with mummy tummies is because they don't isolate the right muscles. According to Tupler, crunches attack the *rectus abdominis*, that bit that sits on top of everything and presents itself as a "six-pack" once blubber has been shed. To get your prebaby belly back, you need to tackle the muscles beneath the six-pack zone first, especially if you have a separation of the abdominal wall known as *diastasis recti*.

And news flash! You probably do have a diastasis recti; it's estimated that more than 90 percent of pregnant women and new moms have it to some degree. Basically, it's a split right down the middle of your rectus muscle. Without diastasis, the two sides of the rectus are joined together, but once the uterus starts to expand, all that stretching can cause the rectus to separate. FYI, some newborns, especially preemies whose body parts haven't fully developed yet, can also have this condition. Rest assured that it's an utterly, completely normal byproduct of pregnancy and isn't dangerous in any way. It makes achieving rock-hard abs a struggle but it certainly isn't anything to fret about from a health perspective.

A doctor can determine whether, and to what degree, you have a diastasis. Or you can attempt to find out for yourself using Tupler's method: Try to push your fingers between your stomach muscles just below your belly button. If you're successful—meaning you can push your fingers in—you have a diastasis. Per Tupler, I have a small one.

Whether a diastasis can be corrected through exercise is hotly debated. Not surprisingly, some plastic surgeons think a full-blown tummy tuck is the only way to get rid of it. But at least there's a mini consensus on one point: Doing the wrong exercise can make your stomach poochier than ever, producing exactly the opposite of the effect you're after.

Pilates

Even Pilates, which enjoys a well-deserved reputation as a tummy trimmer, needs to be approached carefully postpartum. According to expert Erika Bloom, only "contemporary" Pilates will fill the bill. The other main type of Pilates—"classical"—can actually exacerbate a diastasis. "Basically, 'classical' Pilates has been turned into something Joe Pilates never intended," says Bloom. "It's a lot of flexion and reps just focusing on the *rectus abdominis* muscle. That's not going to do anything to make someone's stomach look flatter, and it's actually dangerous for prenatal and postnatal women. The way the core is supposed to be addressed in Pilates—specifically with prenatal and postnatal clients—is by engaging the deeper muscles."

In technical terms, Bloom is talking about the *multifidus, transversus abdominis*, and *psoas*, all of which are situated under the rectus. "Those are the muscles that are the most stretched out and weakened from carrying the baby and giving birth," she says. "If you don't get those back in shape, you'll actually run the risk of a dropped uterus, of incontinence, and of the digestive system not functioning well." In other words, the importance of strengthening your core extends far beyond looking hot in a bikini again.

If you can't make it to a contemporary Pilates class designed especially for new moms, working out at home is another option, but only with a postnatal DVD (see my recommendations in the Dig Deeper Appendix). Or consider splurging on a private session with a contemporary instructor to devise a personalized routine that's both effective and safe.

Another option is to crack open Tupler's *Mummy Tummy* book, which presents an array of exercises for strengthening the transverse muscle. Resting well beneath the rectus, the transverse is a horizontal muscle that functions as a sort of natural corset. Two of my favorites from Tupler's arsenal are the "Flattener Five" and the "Pulse," the instructions for which are in her book and are also included in Mama Mio's "Bootcamp For Tummies" kit (*www.mamamio.com*). I won't try to explain them here, but will vouch for the fact that they're easy and super convenient because you can do them sitting upright anywhere there's a chair to plop your fanny in.

Of course, for every Bloom and Tupler, there are other fitness gurus, including Kirsch and Chabut, who still believe in traditional stomach moves. I know, I know—there are so many schools of thought on this it's enough to give you an instant migraine. Especially when you consider that no exercise will spot reduce your tummy (or any other body part). The goal is to strengthen and tone your midsection so you have a solid foundation for hoisting your baby in and out of car seats and strollers and on and off the changing table. And you'll fare better with any stomach-strengthening plan, and see faster results, if you keep yourself at a good weight with lots of cardio.

So please accept my apologies for throwing so many opinions, so much information, and an entire stomach anatomy lesson at you. But I think it's important to realize that you can do six-pack-type exercises until the cows come home and not get anywhere. What busy mama bear has time for that? None I know of.

hope in a jar, part 1

Even if you lucked out on the diastasis front, I'm still willing to bet the skin on your belly is less than perfect: slack, crêpe-like with a texture similar to an orange peel, perhaps marred by stretch marks. Patricia, mama of twins, says, "In the beginning, I remember looking at my stomach in disgust and awe. It's mostly the same size as before delivering, but the texture is just completely different—very mushy and soft." If this sounds like you, welcome to the club. Yes, I'm a member, although I miraculously escaped stretch marks.

Cue the ever-expanding fleet of stomach firmers! The goal of a firming cream is to, at least temporarily, drain excess fluid from fatty tissues, thereby giving you a sleeker look. A host of natural extracts like horsetail, seaweed, and green tea along with caffeine, which functions as a diuretic, are typical ingredients deployed to make this happen.

Although I'm skeptical that any topically applied potion can shrink your stomach by inches, some of the newer body-firming products are just so rich and chock full of skin-beautifying goodies that it really makes sense to use them in lieu of a cheapie body lotion that merely hydrates. Now that you've had a baby, the skin on your belly has just flat out changed, and it deserves a little TLC. "When it comes to skincare, women are so fixated on the face," says Tanya Mackay, marketing whiz of Mama Mio, which recently added a body-slimming product called "Get Waisted" to its lineup of pregnancy and postpartum skin beautifiers. "But we're focused on this part," she says, gesturing to that vast, often-neglected expanse between the neck and the knees. "Why wouldn't you want the skin on your body to be taut, toned, and healthy?" Yeah, why wouldn't you? I certainly do.

industrial-strength undies, your new bf

My own mama was rail thin. We're talking seriously skinny; like 5'6" under 100 pounds skinny. Despite that, she wore a girdle every day of her life, even if it was broiling outside. Why? A few reasons: One, she came of age in the Frank Sinatra era and never quite shook her penchant for tight pencil skirts and the trappings that go along with them, such as stockings and girdles. Two, after having five kids in fairly rapid succession, she just wasn't about to let it all hang out.

Although nobody calls 'em girdles anymore, those stretchy instruments of torture are more popular than ever. In fact, in recent years, there's been a veritable explosion in "shapewear," underpinnings ranging from control-top briefs to head-to-toe onesies that are designed to hold the line on flab and provide a sleeker look under clothes. There's even a line developed by a plastic surgeon, which is pretty genius, if you think about it.

Though my mother would roll over in her grave if she knew this, I only don shapewear when it's absolutely necessary, like if I'm wearing a knit dress that would get me arrested if I didn't anchor the flesh beneath it. I know it's wildly popular, but for me, shapewear has proved to be more of an incentive to cool it with the cookies and cake than something I'm willing to incorporate into my wardrobe on a daily basis. But if it gives you an extra shot of confidence, by all means go for it. And know that my mama is cheering you on from heaven.

reserve the right to . . .

. . . throw yourself a massive pity party because your bikini days are firmly behind you. Once you've had a good cry, hop online or head to your favorite boutique or department store and stock up on a few drop-dead gorgeous one pieces. Opt for styles that play to your best (nontummy) features, such as long legs or toned arms and shoulders.

stepping into the surgical suite

We've now officially entered Drastic Measures Territory, the place you might consider heading when you've really, really tried to tackle a still-poochy belly on your own through fitness and diet and you're still bummed out every time you catch a glimpse of your gut in a mirror or—my own personal tear inducer—summer vacation photos. So in this section, you'll be learning all about liposuction, tummy tucks, and a kind of Chinese menu assortment procedure called the "Mommy Makeover."

Plastic surgery would be fab if it weren't for a few minor drawbacks: It often requires oh-so-scary general anesthesia; it costs a small fortune; the recovery can be brutal; and it puts you out of commission for a while. Other than that, it's really great.

Before you get your knickers in a twist, know that I've had cosmetic surgery myself. (You'll get the 411 on that in the next chapter.) So if you're at your wits' end with your belly and are considering going under the knife—or fat-sucking cannula, as is the case with liposuction—I would never dream of trying to discourage you. As a matter of fact, I recently saw some before-and-after "ab rehab" pictures at a presentation given by one of the top surgeons in New York, and I was blown away. Clearly, lipo and tummy tucks, if done well, can produce fantastic results.

the**mother**load

"My stomach is definitely poochier postbaby, and while I don't mind the extra padding, I don't want to add to it, either. So I try to stay away from foods that promote bloat, especially salt and soda. Since I rarely have time to hit the gym now, I'm much more aware of how much I eat. And because I tend to eat whatever is in front of me, I've tried to implement pretty strict portion controls. For example, I have a small box of Cheerios for breakfast (60 calories) and at lunch I stick to salad in a small container, with a half-ladle of balsamic vinaigrette. And no "empty" calories like white bread or chips—as much as I may crave them."

—Jenny B., mama of one

But surgery is no walk in the park and should only be up for discussion when you're completely sure you've exhausted all your exercise and diet options and made a firm decision not to have any more kids. While the first point holds true for both procedures, the no-more-babies clause really only applies to a tummy tuck. Although it's possible to carry a pregnancy to term after you've had an abdominoplasty (the official moniker for a tummy tuck), it isn't ideal.

Lipo

Because a tummy tuck is a much bigger deal, surgically speaking, why don't more postpartum women just opt for lipo? Good question. Here's the answer: Because the results will usually be less than optimal on a stretched-to-smithereens après-baby belly. According to plastic surgeon Michael Kane, MD, removing fat from beneath reams of skin will wind up looking worse than if you'd done nothing at all. He says, "When we're talking about the abdomen, the ability of liposuction to do anything good goes down abruptly when a woman has had a child. If a woman hasn't had a child, and she's complaining about a little extra fat in her abdomen, I know liposuction is probably going to do something good for her about 90 percent of the time. Once she's had a kid, that number drops to 40 or 50 percent. There are a lot of variables in all of these procedures, but the sole determining variable in how much liposuction can help someone is how much extra skin they have in ratio to the amount of fat you're taking out. After a pregnancy, not only is the skin stretched, it also tends to be thinner and of lower quality. It's less elastic, so it's not as likely to snap back. So any fat you remove will make that excess hanging skin look worse."

When you consider it, that makes perfect sense. Lipo sucks fat, not skin. Think of what all those contestants on "The Biggest Loser" have to contend with. To a lesser extent, postpregnancy is a similar scenario to one in which a person sheds a great deal of weight and then has to deal with the droopy aftermath. Either that slack skin gets sliced off or it lingers indefinitely. After reading all that, I trust you'll agree that, with lipo, it's a buyer-beware scenario.

Tummy Tuck

Plan B is the biggie—a full-blown tummy tuck, which entails, per Dr. Kane, removing "a great big ellipse of skin that was stretched out from the pregnancy, basically from the belly button to the pubic area." According to Dr. Kane, tummy tucks require a hip-to-hip incision so that skin can be lifted all the way up to the rib cage (ouch!). At this point, the *diastasis recti,* which Kane believes all postpartum women have to some degree, is corrected by literally pulling the two halves of the rectus muscle back together and anchoring it with permanent stitches. "We start all the way up at the rib cage, right where the bones are, and from there, right down to the pubic bone, we use a really thick, heavy stitch that doesn't absorb. It's really like fixing a hernia and pulling the sides of the rectus back together in the midline." Not surprisingly, the recovery is lengthy. If you're in the workforce, you can bank on taking two full weeks off. And it could be several months before you're feeling like "you" again.

Mini Tummy Tuck

Unbeknownst to moi before I started my postbaby detective work, there's a middle ground between liposuction and an abdominoplasty. It's called a "mini tummy tuck," and it's a procedure Dr. Kane is keen on for the right candidates. "The 'mini' is an in-betweener operation for the woman who maybe has some *diastasis recti* but for whom it isn't severe and is mostly confined to the lower abdomen," he says. According to Dr. Kane, the "mini" combines elements of liposuction and a full-blown tummy tuck. First, the surgeon removes a substantial amount of fat across the top and along the sides of the abdomen via liposuction. Next, a small incision is made in the vicinity of where a C-section cut is made—an inch or two below the top of your pubic hair. The skin is then lifted up from the belly button down to the pubic area, correcting the *diastasis recti* with a heavy internal stitch. Finally, remaining loose skin—usually just a small wedge—in the area is removed and you're stitched up externally. While that sounds like plenty of cutting and pasting, Dr. Kane says the downtime after a mini tuck is fairly short, with most recipients heading back to work after about a week.

The Mommy Makeover

Before I sign off on this emotionally charged topic, I just want to address one last matter, the "Mommy Makeover." In recent years, this megaprocedure, which bundles a breast augmentation with lipo and a tummy tuck, has been all over the news. The "selling point," if you will, is that you're overhauling everything that's bothering you in one fell swoop. Depending on who's doing the operating, it's also sometimes presented as a cost-saving measure—primarily because it's a single block of time with the anesthesiologist, use of the surgical suite, etc. And for sure, you can find happy campers on the message boards of plastic-surgery websites extolling the virtues of the Mommy Makeover. But is it just me, or does this sound like the very definition of hell? I can only imagine the pain following an überoperation like that, akin to recovering from a massive car crash, one assumes. Certainly gives new meaning to the term "suffering for beauty."

If your ears perked up at the mention of the breast augmentation in the Mommy Makeover (even if you'd never, in a million years, go that route yourself), you're going to love the next chapter, which is all about dealing with less-than-perky postbaby boobs.

Ditching Diet Coke

Okay, Diet Coke. Can we just say biggest oxymoron ever? There's nothing remotely "diet" about a chemical-laden liquid (albeit one that tastes fantastic and is utterly addictive in its fantabulosity) that puffs you up bigger than a hot-air balloon. As soon as I cut that tasty-yet-toxic beverage out of my life after my second skin-cancer scare (it took the threat of death to get me off the dime), I lost four pounds that have stayed off ever since. To boot, my belly is flatter, and trust me when I tell you it's not because of extra ab work.

In place of my beloved Diet Coke, I've started drinking more water. At least during the week, that is. Somehow running to the bathroom to pee every ten minutes just seems to make the workday go faster. Still, even though I'm obsessed with the slightest weight loss, I didn't really connect the dots between zapping the Diet Coke, imbibing more H20, and shedding a little blubber.

According to nutrition expert Jackie Keller, all those gazillion bubbles are to blame for the fact that bevvies that purport to slim you down actually do quite the opposite. "When you're trying to debloat, the first thing to do is to get rid of carbonated sodas. And the fact that you substituted water rather than another carbonated beverage means you probably put your body back in a better hydrated state. And maybe, subconsciously, because you're better hydrated, you're actually eating less," she says. "A lot of times we eat when we're really thirsty. We don't realize that the thirst mechanism is pretty dull, and we don't always recognize thirst for what it is. Sometimes we think thirst is hunger, so we eat when we don't really need to. When you rehydrate yourself, you no longer have that unjustified hunger."

I'll drink to that. Just not with Diet Coke.

breast intentions

Next to a less-than-stellar stomach, boobs typically rank at the top of our collective "this-is-*so*-not-cool" postbaby figure complaints. For now, we'll put aside the psychological stuff (i.e., the transformation of your once-perky man magnets into a utilitarian milking machine) and focus on the specifics of what's going on and how to make the best of it. Lord knows the gripes I hear are infinite. From my skinny-minny friends, the beef is that what little boobage they had prepregnancy has gone missing entirely. On the other end of the spectrum—a far more populated place to hang out, by the way—the chief woe is that there's just way too much rack happening, especially in those early postpartum months when breastfeeding is a 24/7 situation.

Both scenarios can seriously mess with your self-confidence. Happily, there are tricks and tips (and surgery, if you're so inclined) to help you regain your sense of sexy. Just read on and don't look down for a spell.

cups runneth over

We live in a country that worships at the altar of big boobs, but having a baby often delivers more than we bargained for in that regard. Sure, that first trimester swelling is pretty exciting, and I'll bet that if you were in good shape heading into your pregnancy, you felt gorgeous. Think about it: Your hair was lush from the prenatal vitamins, your skin was glowing, and what little tummy pooch you had at that point filled out your stretchy tops and spandex little black dresses beautifully. I remember feeling really sexy in the initial months of preggodom. Like wolf-whistles-in-the-street sexy.

Flashforward to the third and "fourth" trimesters, and it's a very different story. Your rack is now enormous and, let's be honest, probably not in a hot way. Yes, your breasts are there for a reason; one of the best ones there is, nourishing your newborn. But I'd venture to say that, for most women, having a little less up top would go a long way in boosting postpartum body image. Unless you've got a fairly slim waist, hips, and ass, giant breasts just read "old lady." And sadly, what goes up (and out and over) must come down.

reserve the right to . . .

. . . stop comparing yourself to every rack that crosses your sight-lines, whether it's at the playground or in the pages of *Us Magazine*. Just because the entire planet is boob obsessed doesn't mean you have to be. Issue a new-mom moratorium on all that and free your mind for more important stuff.

next stop, sag central

Since I've pointed the finger at my DD for virtually every health and beauty woe I've even thought of since she came into my life, you can imagine how fast I tried to pin droopy breasts on her, too. I figured that whatever little breastfeeding and pumping I did was the chief reason behind my plummet in perkiness, despite the fact that I switched to formula after one month.

I'm not the only one blaming my DD for my woes, though. In fact, I have plenty of company on the floppy front. "My boobs are straight out of *National Geographic*," says Ninka, mama of two. "Seriously saggy and deflated, as if I'd never worn a bra in my entire life. Remember the 'pencil test?' I could probably hold a dozen hostage under these suckers." (Note to the young 'uns: Google "Pencil Test" and grab an unsharpened Number 2. . . .)

But as it turns out, nursing—whether it was the paltry month I eked out or the hardcore two-kids-for-a-year-each type that Ninka did—apparently isn't to blame for deflation. As at least one reputable study has determined, there is no definitive link between breastfeeding and *ptosis*, the medical term for the sagging of the boob. Which isn't to say our wee ones are off the hook completely; evidently, pregnancy itself is a contributing factor, and the more times you're pregnant, the more drooping you can expect. That's primarily due to the weight fluctuation that occurs, which stretches the skin. Yet another reason to bag unhealthy yo-yo dieting that stretches your figure in and out like an accordion.

Other causes include aging and, oddly enough, smoking. It seems the chemicals in cancer sticks are responsible for a breakdown in elastin, the protein that supports the skin. And while sunbathing and indoor tanning weren't cited in the study as potential sag inducers, those nasty little habits also beat the smithereens out of elastin and collagen. Sure, most American women don't lay out topless, at least not in public. But anyone who's ever used a tanning bed (and yes, tragically, I'm one of them) typically does so sans bikini top.

So unless you want to remain childless (oops, too late for that), never smoke a single cigarette in your entire life or allow a ray of ultraviolet light to touch your chest—and somehow, Dorian Gray-like, refuse to age—your breasts are going to head south at some point. Your choice now is to either accept your fate in a Zen-like fashion or attempt to fight sagginess with an arsenal of temporary and semipermanent solutions.

If you're leaning toward Option A, I'd heartily recommend a visit to the überempowering website The Shape of a Mother (*www.theshapeofamother.blogspot.com*), where you'll see myriad images of postpartum women happy to reveal their après-baby bodies and share their postpartum tales.

For proactive types—and that can range from anyone who just wants to corral those wayward boobs a bit to those of you who are seriously mourning the memory of your sixteen-year-old, prenewborn knockers—read on.

lift your spirits (along with that rack)

There's the instant route to a perkier pair (a kick-ass bra) and the slower, see-results-over-time method, which entails shedding weight globally and hitting the gym or living room, dumbbells in hand, for spot work. Personally, I swear by all of these approaches.

Undergarments

First the seemingly easy part: supportive, flattering undergarments. This is so huge, but mysteriously, shockingly difficult. Why else would an estimated 85 percent of American women be wearing the wrong size? (For websites that provided guidance on proper fitting, see the Dig Deeper Appendix.)

Since I detest the feeling of underwires, which many women adore for their ability to hoist their breasts heavenward, I'm at a slight disadvantage in the uplifting-bra arena. Instead, I rely on the "smoosh it all down" approach with soft-cup minimizers, like my beloved Sassybax. If you're not familiar with Sassybax, they're these great stretchy, hardware-free upper-body shapers that rein in not only your boobs, but loathsome back fat, too, thereby killing two birds with one stone. My only gripe with Sassybax is that they're a little pricey. So if you're on a budget and prefer to go underwireless like me, consider looking into the soft-cup minimizer offerings by Bali, Valmont, and Lilyette.

the**mother**load

"I invested some time and money in a proper bra-fitting session and bought all new postnursing bras. This is one of the best wardrobe investments I've made—what a difference a great bra makes! I also make sure to do regular chest exercises a few times a week like flys or push-ups. Doing just a few goes a long way to supporting your bust and keeping things firm."

—Mara, mama of two

If you're an underwire lover, be sure to note that there is no industry standard for the shape of the underwire itself, so you really need to shop around to find the brand you feel most comfortable in—especially now, when you might be packing a little extra boobage. With all you've got going on, the last thing you want is that annoying feeling of a too-tight underwire digging into you. With a properly fitting bra, you shouldn't be able to sense an underwire at all. (By the way, my mama spies tell me that Barely There makes very comfy underwire styles.)

But whatever you decide to wear or pay, it's money well spent. "My 34Bs have weathered the storm pretty well," says twins mama

Christine. "They're a little bit deflated, but not so bad. I do find that my old flimsy bras with no underwire or structure just don't hack it anymore. I've had to splurge on a few new ones, but that was actually a nice treat." So don't shy away from shopping for a few frisky new bras that give you a real lift, physically and otherwise. It's not like you're breaking the bank for a fur coat!

Shed a Pound or Two

My other game plan is to slim down globally, which has definitely helped the postbaby boob situation. I'm now back to my pre-DD weight, and the overall effect is a lot less chesty. Of course, that's also because I had my implants removed, a tale I'll get to in a moment. But I don't want to sell myself too short here. I've worked my ass off—through both tons of cardio and rewiring my eating habits—to trim five freaking pounds. But on a shrimp such as myself, a handful of flab makes a big difference. (To learn how I did it, see "Worked for Me.") I know that each of you has your own "magic number," the weight at which your body confidence skyrockets. Why not go for it?

While you're at it, be sure to toss a few pec exercises into your workout routine. Moves that target the pectorals will help correct breast sagging by strengthening the underlying chest muscles. Big bonus: your posture will improve, too.

Until I had a baby, I never fully appreciated the beauty of a good dumbbell fly. Think of them as a bench press with hand weights. Because I don't have an adjustable weight bench in my house (yet), I just use my husband's piano bench. Remember the hot-mama theme song: No excuses!

hope in a jar, part 2

In addition to melt-in-your-mouth croissants, the French are responsible for adding the concept of décolleté care to our beauty regimens. Now, along with the elaborate, multistep bust-firming treatments now available at better spas throughout the U.S., cosmetics counters are now teeming with little pots of boob cream.

As long as you're not breastfeeding, I don't see anything wrong with using a bust-firming décolleté cream. Many top American beauty companies have added them to their lineups, including Estée Lauder. And I happen to love Boob Tube by Mama Mio, which is super rich and contains zero dodgy ingredients such as phthalates, parabens, or synthetic fragrances. I figure if I'm rubbing anything directly into my chest, I want it to be as free of possibly carcinogenic chemicals as possible. Call me paranoid, but I'm taking every precaution I can to avoid becoming another breast-cancer statistic.

Now that I've broached that scary topic, I'd have to say that the best reason to add a bust-firming cream to your ritual is not smoother, softer skin but rather that it gets you in touch with your boobs on a regular basis. Hopefully, you're all doing a monthly self-exam (please, please, please assure me that you are). Well, adding a breast firmer ups the ante on lump detection, reason alone to dip your paws into that jar.

the knife point: pros and cons of surgery

Okay, so we're back in drastic-measures country. While I can completely relate to wanting to plunk down cold, hard cash in an effort to bump Ma Nature aside and reshape your breasts via surgery, I've already gone that route, and I have to say I didn't especially love it.

Here's the backstory: In my early thirties, after going on a long shoot with a photographer and a crew of models who didn't eat meat, I became a vegetarian. It wasn't some crazy whim, but rather something I'd been contemplating for a while. Once I saw how easy it could be, I took the plunge. But between going meat free and enduring the heartbreak of a few tumultuous pre-Hubby relationships, I shed ten pounds from my already lean, 5'1" frame. That brought me down, at one point, to a measly, somewhat unhealthy, eighty-nine pounds. What little boobage I had to begin with went completely AWOL. And although flat-as-a-pancake, seventeen-year-old Kate Moss was at the apex of her hotness at that time—and I worked at a fashion magazine that was all about that kind of waify, zonked-out, "heroin chic"—I just felt that I, personally, looked like a child. A woman trapped in a little girl's body.

I know most shrinks would have a field day with that semi-warped, playing-into-the-beauty-myth self-assessment. Mine certainly did. But I still went for it. And I'd have to admit that the psychological impact of merely bumping up one cup size—from a skimpy A to a B—was substantial. Instantly, those little-girl feelings disappeared. There was also symmetry happening for the first time in my postadolescent life. I'd always had a small waist and (relatively) large hips. Now, with something on top, the hourglass was complete.

I had implants for more than a decade and they didn't give me an ounce of trouble. I experienced none of the horror stories you hear about like hardening, deflation, etc. Placed beneath the pectoral muscles, they were also tastefully un-stripper like. So what was the problem, you ask? I just got bored. A flatter aesthetic was beckoning to me, but by the time I was officially "over" my implants, I was also trying to get pregnant. Not wanting to upset the physical applecart with elective surgery until after I'd had a baby, I postponed my dream of returning to Pancake Land. As soon as I felt up to it postdelivery, out they came.

Now back to you. Obviously, as someone who's had implants, I won't be raining on your parade if you're longing to get them. But I'm also not going to nudge you in that direction, either. Consider me the Switzerland of fake boobs—neutral, although, if I could rewind the tape on my life, I'd skip them and find peace with the little morsels I was given. (Oh, and for the record, my natural flatness wasn't imaginary; I recently had drinks with an old college chum who, when the topic drifted toward cosmetic surgery said, "You had *nothing* up there. I mean *nothing*." Um, thanks. . . .)

As for the two other main types of breast surgery—reductions and lifts—while I can't vouch for them personally, I can see why they'd be a compelling proposition. In particular, reductions seem pretty life changing.

Just promise me you'll do tons of research, that you'll interview several highly credentialed, board-certified prospective surgeons, and that you'll commit the pros and cons below to memory before you make your decision. And sorry to be a killjoy, but there are quite a few more cons than pros.

The Upside:

- Enhanced self-esteem and better body image
- Clothes fit better (as long as new cup size is kept in proportion to the rest of your body)

The Downside:

- Requires general anesthesia or IV sedation coupled with local anesthesia
- Lengthy, initially painful recovery period (worse if implants are placed below pec muscles)
- Potential scarring (particularly with reductions and lifts)
- Temporary (and possibly permanent) loss of nipple sensation
- Possibility of capsular contraction (i.e., hardening) or deflation with implants
- Results are not permanent; sagging will reappear over time and implants, which are not "lifelong" devices, will need to be removed or replaced at some point
- Future breastfeeding could be compromised
- Cost (varies widely, but usually runs at least ten grand)

Of course, despite all the ground we've just covered, it isn't written in stone that there will be boob aftermath for every new mom. And if you're pregnant while you're reading this, don't do any pre-emptive, jump the gun-style fretting and fussing. "Once I was done breastfeeding, I was happy to see that my boobs went back to normal," says mama Jill S. "I'm in the minority and absolutely love having nearly nonexistent boobs—seriously, they're like AA size. And I assume that'll happen again after I'm done feeding baby number two." See how she's thinking positively? Love that!

Gwen, a mama of two who turns fifty this year, is also a perfectly happy camper. "My boobs are the best part of my body," she reports. "Although gravity has taken its toll elsewhere, they're still 'up there' and look great."

Whatever your boobs happen to look like right now, do what you can to improve their appearance and then try to just chillax about the whole thing. Remember, your DD thinks you're fine just the way you are!

worked for me!

Slimming Down

After I parted company with the implants, I was expecting (and hoping) to be Kate Hudson flat. But though there was definitely less boobage, that didn't happen, and for a while there, I was perplexed. Then it finally dawned on me: After all those years of mindless noshing—and delivering a big old baby to boot—I was fifteen pounds heavier than I was when I got them. Time to get serious.

It's an ongoing journey, and I'm still not where I'd eventually like to be. But thanks to saying buh-bye to my beloved Diet Coke and incorporating tips from the book (details in the Dig Deeper Appendix), *10 Habits That Mess Up a Woman's Diet,* I've lost several pounds. So here's what I'm doing differently:

- I eat breakfast every morning, no matter how crazed I am.
- I make a conscious attempt to step up the fruit and veggie consumption.
- I snack meaningfully twice a day (read: no vending machines).
- I practice "portion vigilance" by reading labels and learning to "eyeball" foods.
- I recognize that every bite—a morsel of cookie, a half-pat of butter—adds up.
- I stop eating when I'm full, even when the food is incredible.

Until I reach my ultimate goal, I'll continue to smoosh with my Sassybax. Oh, and there's one last great-rack trick I finally learned: excellent posture. By throwing your shoulders back, straightening your spine, and tucking your bum under a bit, it's like an instant breast lift and tummy tuck. See, our mama bears were really onto something when they told us to stand up straight.

the power of primping

I'm not home much on weekday afternoons, so sadly, I'm utterly *Oprah* deprived. But one day, about the time I was contemplating morphing *Momover* from an online column into the snappy little book you're holding in your mitts right now, I happened to catch one of the makeover episodes.

The women selected for top-to-bottom overhauls struck me the hardest. In "before" tape after "before" tape, they just kept yapping about the main reason they'd let themselves go: Because they'd had kids. It was so frustrating to hear them chatter about how their newly shifted priorities meant their blush and lipstick were off in a cabinet somewhere, covered in cobwebs. You could just feel them yearning to recapture a little of their prebaby babedom. Of course Oprah's crack team rescued them, at least for the day. But I couldn't help thinking that if they didn't start off with a mental Momover, followed in short order by a physical Momover, they'd be headed right back to Frumpy Town as soon as they left that Windy City studio. I won't let that happen to you.

burn the sweatpants, relocate the eyelash curler

On the Momover continuum, there's a time to ease up on yourself and a time to step up your game. But what's cool about the fashion and beauty thing—as opposed to, say, making sure you're eating your veggies and cranking through all those damn workouts—is that making a bit of extra effort is fun. It feels good to sneak off to the bathroom, lock the door, and start fussing with the tinted moisturizer and straightening iron. So why in the world would you deny yourself a bit of pleasure in a day crammed with chores and responsibilities, especially when the payoff is so big? After all, by allowing yourself a mere fifteen minutes to buff and polish every day, you're not only instantly lowering your stress level, you're sending "Mom Matters" signals all over the place.

Before we talk skincare and makeup, a brief word about your postpartum wardrobe. With so many how-to books about fashion cramming store shelves (not to mention television shows like TLC's *What Not to Wear*), I won't dwell on clothes too much here, except to say this: There's a whole geometry thing happening that I didn't know about before I started researching a massive body-types story

I wrote for *Glamour* a few years back. Seriously, there's a reason why a tiny person like moi looks best in monotones, skinny belts, small prints, etc.

After birthing your bambina, your own personal geometry has probably shifted somewhat. So do yourself a favor and nab one of my favorite fashion-advice books listed in the Dig Deeper Appendix. And yes, burn the sweatpants, but not before you make sure you have something else to wear instead! Often it's just a matter of "shopping your closet" and pulling together outfits that flatter your (temporarily) curvier postbaby body.

pick your battles

It's my theory (honed by twenty years as a beauty editor, but a theory nonetheless) that most of us have a list of primping non-negotiables, those imaginary lines in the sand that we never cross. For Christine, it's great skin. She's even ramped up her regime in her quest for a more flawless complexion. "I got this thing called a Vi peel which really helped get rid of extra pigment," she says. "I had tried to get pregnant for so long that I avoided a lot of the more potent beauty treatments like Retin-A, and now I find that I'm taking better care of my skin than I did before. It's more of a priority. If I have great skin, then I'll spend less time on makeup. It works out in the end. I can just wash my face, put on some lip balm, and leave the house and I don't feel like a hag." (FYI, this woman is categorically incapable of looking like a hag, but you get the basic drift.)

For me, it's roots; I can't abide seeing any tell-tale signs of regrowth, so I'm in that salon swivel chair every month like clockwork regardless of what's going on in my life. Conversely, there are aspects of beauty upkeep that I couldn't care less about, like getting a weekly mani. I just keep my nails super short and my hands semi-moisturized and call it a day. Summer feet, however, are a different story. From Memorial Day until the leaves start falling from the trees, I'm all about pristine, pedicured toes painted in dusty pink shades, à la Essie's "Starter Wife."

reserve the right to . . .

. . . sequester yourself in the bathroom for a quick makeup job, even before a trip to the local diner for your weekly Saturday morning pancake fest. Though my own weekend routine is super basic (concealer, bronzing powder, and lipgloss), I never let Hubby or the DD rush me out of it.

But I digress; it's you we're talking about here. As a new mama, your list of "musts" is undoubtedly a whole lot shorter than it was prebaby. It has to be, unless you want to hire live-in help to mind the tot while you zip around town from one beauty appointment to the next. Therefore, you'll need to suss out what's most important to you as far as your looks and keep at it. You may shift to DIY in some cases (we'll get to self-maintenance shortly), but you'll still need to determine what makes you feel pretty, hot, or even pretty hot.

Like my roots fixation, hair probably tops many a new-mom beauty agenda. By all means, keep up with those appointments if they give you a lift and help you feel on top of all things you. There's nothing worse than wanting to shriek every time you catch a glimpse of yourself in the mirror. Still, you might just decide to . . .

embrace covert low maintenance

When I was at *Cookie,* trying to map out the best approach to covering the insanely massive beauty market for our time-pressed— but still appearance-conscious—new-mom readers, I kept coming back around to this notion of covert low maintenance: stuff that seems like a massive time suck or pain in the ass that secretly isn't.

Like growing your hair halfway down your back. Although it seems easier to just hack it all off after the baby arrives—the old "mom chop" cliché—short hair typically has to be styled to look halfway decent. What's so low maintenance about that?

Professional peels, like the ones Christine gets, are another example of covert low maintenance. I'm a big fan of these, too, although I've shifted, après DD, from four times a year to two. In between appointments, I supplement with acid-drenched pads I get from my dermatologist. (Great ones for you to try include MD Skincare Alpha Beta Daily Face Peel, *www.mdskincare.com*.)

If you want better skin but are just way too exhausted at the end of a long day to do a thorough job of cleansing and applying antiaging night cremes and whatnot, try to do it early, as in right after you get in from the office or after dinner if you're a stay-at-home mom. The temptation to blow it off will be greatly reduced by getting it out of the way long before you start nodding off in front of the TV. I've also started slipping a little covert low maintenance into my getting ready for work routine. For example, I find that taking just a little extra time to do my makeup pays off in spades (read how in "Worked for Me").

I could go on and on about covert low maintenance, but remember, the point is not to immediately dismiss a technique, procedure, or product just because it seems like a huge effort. Whatever it is could wind up being the most time-efficient aspect of your entire beauty regime.

when—and when not—to diy

I happen to live in a city that's home to some of the most famous beauty gurus in the world. Does that mean I'm running off to a salon or spa every five seconds? Hardly. In fact, since becoming a mommy, I'm committed to learning to do more and more stuff for myself. Still, some things are best left to professionals. Here's a rundown of what is and isn't doable *chez* you.

Hair Trims

This drives me bananas: One week my hair will be such a perfect length and shape that I want to freeze frame it. Then a mere week later, it's all I can do not to grab the scissors and start whacking. But when shears are involved, there isn't a lot to be done at home without suffering major consequences. So stick with the small stuff. For example, trimming your own bangs is fine, says salon owner Anthony Gianzero, my colorist of fifteen years. Just be sure to cut while hair is dry not wet, because of the "shrinkage" factor. And rather than attempting a straight-across fringe, angle the scissors slightly while cutting into the hair, snipping just a bit at a time. That way it looks more grownup, less American Girl doll.

However, as much as they might need it, trimming your own split ends isn't a great idea. "It's almost impossible to get the back straight on your own," says Gianzero. "Even pulling the hair away from the head just slightly will result in layers." And he's not talking the lush, Elle Macpherson kind of layers, either.

Color and Highlights

A general rule of thumb is that if you're going darker or trying to match your natural brunette locks, home coloring is usually fine. "There's a lot of science to great color, but some women get okay results with a box dye," says Gianzero. "It all depends on the look you're trying to achieve." Once you get into any type of lightening, however, you're much better off heading to the salon. "You should never bleach at home," he says.

Skin Treatments

Recently, there's been a surge in the beauty "device" category—small handheld contraptions meant to replicate procedures you'd get at a spa or dermatologist's office. There are also tons of do-it-yourself kits designed to make your skin glow like a Christmas tree. In theory, they're a great idea for new moms, especially in those first few months when you're welded to your tot, but because they aren't cheap, it's important to do a bit of reconnaissance work before plunking down the plastic. To aid your decision making, I called überdermatologist Fredric Brandt and quizzed him about some of the more popular home fixer uppers. If you choose to partake, go easy. "No matter what you're doing, there's a potential to overstrip the skin," says Dr. Brandt. "Especially in winter months, when you want to keep the epidermal barrier intact. Don't overdo it."

Clarisonic Skin Care Brush

Created by the same folks who brought you the Sonicare tooth-brush, this electric complexion gizmo purports to remove makeup six times better than your regular manual routine, which (theoretically) leaves behind mega dirt and oil that gets trapped in pores. Basically, it functions like a plug-in facial. "I think they're great if you wear a lot of makeup and want to thoroughly cleanse your skin," says Dr. Brandt. "And there are some studies that show if you use a Clarisonic brush, cremes will penetrate more deeply. But I'm not sure that a thorough washing wouldn't achieve the same effect." For more info, visit *www.clarisonic.com*.

Laser and LED Devices

By harnessing laser beams or light-emitting diodes (LEDs) into a handheld unit, these gadgets address beauty concerns ranging from acne and unwanted hair to lines and wrinkles. "They're like a less intense version of the Gentle Waves procedure we do in the office, which opens the pores," says Dr. Brandt. "I think the home ver-sion probably does help somewhat, but the big issue is user fatigue. You're not under a big spotlight like you are at a dermatologist's, so you really need to spend a lot of time going over one small area. It's like buying one of those exercise machines you see on TV. How long will you continue to use it and be disciplined about it?" Still, some well-known skin gurus, including derm Nicholas Perricone, have gotten into the act. For a selection of said gadgets, including

Dr. Perricone's Light Renewal, check out the Sephora website at *www.sephora.com.*

Microdermabrasion and Peel Kits

Essentially, these are meant to sweep flaky, dry, "old" skin aside to make room for the newer, dewier variety. While microderm-abrasion physically dislodges "dead" cells via grainy crystals, peels rely on chemicals—typically acids—to achieve the same effect. And they get high marks from Dr. B, who offers both types of products within his own line (*www.drbrandtskincare.com*). "I like them because they increase your cell turnover rate and stimulate the production of collagen. They're also useful for radiance." Rather than a multistep liquid peel, I personally prefer the acid pads I referred to earlier, which I find to be a perfect stopgap between my semiannual trips to the derm for deeper peels.

Teeth

According to dentist to the stars Gregg Lituchy, sky-high estrogen levels are the reason you needed to raise your game with at least three cleanings and massive brushing and flossing during your pregnancy. (You did do that, right?) But you can't slack off after you deliver, either. "The gums become really inflamed and they bleed easily. Those high estrogen levels will stay around while you're breastfeeding, too," Lituchy says. "Unfortunately, a lot of things can fall apart during that time. Because the gums are in bad condition, with plaque building up, you're more prone to decay." Yippy-skippy.

So, now that you know what you must do (be extra vigilant with checkups and scrubbing) here's what you can't do while you're nursing: any type of bleaching or whitening. Lituchy says, "The gums are very vascular, and here you have this peroxide solution that's going to seep through. So I tell my patients not to do any bleaching until they're finished breastfeeding." Still, per the doc, there are things you can do to brighten your smile, like eating crunchy vegetables and brushing your teeth the second you've consumed anything that stains, such as coffee, red wine, or pomegranate juice. And, if you're not breastfeeding, brushing with baking soda mixed with a small amount of hydrogen peroxide will also perk your pearlies right up.

Hair Removal

Earlier in this chapter, I mentioned my obsession with covert low maintenance, and I'd have to say that my prebaby bikini-line electrolysis was a primo example of this. Because I was good and sick of getting ingrown hairs after shaving this area (and I'm just a little body-hair phobic), I cracked open the old piggy bank for electrolysis, which required about twenty hour-long sessions. The upside? I haven't needed a wax in years. For my legs, I'm keen on instant gratification, so I shave every single day of my life. To me, shaving ranks right up there with brushing my teeth in the morning.

Listen, I'm not trying to "overshare" here, and while I don't think there's a mama alive who would want to take the time away from playing kissy face with her precious babe to get bikini-line electrolysis, this all-important grooming category may be worth a little re-evaluation. For instance, if prebaby you were a leg shaver, you might find waxing more of a time saver now. Or vice versa. Read on and make some smart après-delivery choices.

Waxing

Because I'm way too impatient to let the hair on my legs grow in long enough to wax, I don't understand why so many gals are into this. I guess I can understand wanting to do the upper lip, but even in that case, I prefer going to a salon for threading. This ancient Eastern hair-removal technique involves having a cotton thread pulled along the unwanted facial hair, twisting it, trapping it, and ripping it out by the follicle. It sounds a little barbaric, I know, but it's fast, hygienic, and lasts for up to six weeks. And really, on the pain front, threading hurts about as much as waxing, but I find there's less residual redness.

If you're considering waxing at home, Dr. Brandt says it's important to make sure the wax isn't too hot before applying. Also bear in mind that certain topical products can make skin much more sensitive. "If you're using any type of product that strips the *stratum corneum* (the outermost layer of the epidermis) like Retin-A—which you shouldn't be doing if you're breastfeeding, by the way—or any kind of acid like glycolic or salicylic, you can burn your skin with waxing," says Dr. Brandt. Which isn't to say that you shouldn't ever wax, just that it might not be advisable to go it alone.

the**mother**load

"The only maintenance I do on a regular basis is either A) a must (e.g., covering those tell-tale grays—I may be the oldest mom at nursery school, but I refuse to look it) or B) a time saver, like my weekly blow-outs. The fifty minutes I spend getting a shampoo and blow dry save me at least twenty minutes a day of trying to tame my wildly curly hair by myself. Not being more assiduous in my beauty upkeep is almost more guilt inducing than taking the time to do it because as I get older, it's clear that I need to focus on certain, ahem, 'issues.' It's just that when I have the spare time, I would so much rather spend it with my daughter than being fluffed and buffed!"

—**Jenny B.**, mama of one

LASERS

This is where one of those handheld gizmos, like the new No!No! (*www.my-no-no.com*) come into play. By deploying heat to "disrupt the hair growth cycle," with a No!No! or similar type of product (such as Silk'n and Tria), the thinking is that the follicle will eventually cease to exist. Although FDA approved for use all over the body, some dermatologists warn against using an at-home laser on your face. But if you have some extra cash lying around (these devices run from about $250 for a No!No! to approximately $500 for a Silk'n), you may end up saving yourself money in the long run. After all, in-office hair removal costs an average of $150 per session, which can add up pretty quickly.

Mani/Pedi

Maybe I've just read one too many fungus stories, but I've become pretty paranoid about nipping off to the local nail joint for a mani/pedi. However, that actually works out fine because, as I've said, my hands are a polish-free zone. And during the two-and-a-half seasons a year when no one is gazing at my toes, I usually skip pro pedicures, too. Not that I do nothing, though! To deep-six all the rough skin and calluses that accumulate from pounding the New York streets, I use high-test exfoliants spiked with acids, such as DDF Pedi-Cream. I've also been trying to get up to speed with my PedEgg, a "microfile" that essentially functions as a skin grater. One big caveat with the PedEgg, Revlon's Pedi-Expert, or any type of microfile: diabetics need to steer clear. And even nondiabetics shouldn't go too nuts. Remember, your skin is a protective barrier. And while it might be okay to remove a little of the rough stuff, overzealous scraping with a PedEgg or any other type of microfile can quickly cut into healthy, soft skin as well.

As for my hands, I've become addicted to rubbing miracle facial crèmes into them at night just before bed. These creams can seem a little expensive, but I think it's really worth it to "trade up" on the hand-cream front. After all those nappy changes, your poor paws deserve a little TLC.

Okay hot mama, it's time to catch your breath from all that physical care stuff and beautifying. In the next part of the book, you'll be diving into your spiritual and emotional lives. Being super healthy in these areas is crucial to your Momover. So grab a cup of herbal tea, put your feet up, and read on.

worked for me!

Piling It On

Could I be any luckier? When I need beauty advice, I can actually get Sonia Kashuk, one of the best makeup artists in the business, to take my calls. And after I had my tot, my digits were dialing.

First, I wanted to know the best ways to perk up a decidedly unperky complexion. "I'm a big proponent of blush," says Kashuk, a mama of two and close pal of model-mom Cindy Crawford. "No matter how tired you are I'm not one to say, 'Grab the concealer,' because I think a little darkness can actually be sexy. If you have darkness under your eyes and no color in your face, you look dead. But if you're a little dark and you have a flushy glow in your cheeks, you look alive. In my opinion, blush will save you faster than concealer."

Duly noted. I now blush like crazy. Basically, I don't leave the house without it.

Next, I wanted to run my theory past her: that spending more time on my makeup in the morning will actually be more efficient because I won't be running to the bathroom for touchups all day. In other words, more is more.

"Absolutely," she says. "When you take five extra minutes in the morning you look that much more polished and pulled together." And there's nothing I like better than looking polished and pulled together!

"Layering," says Kashuk. "That's another key. And so is using powder, whether it's pressed or loose. Powder is a makeup-bag must have, even if you only use it sparingly." Taking all this into consideration, I devised the following layered-up routine: On a clean, moisturized "canvas," I use stick foundation where needed (around the nose, chin, and any pesky red patches); followed by a dusting of bronzing powder all over; then blush (I like crème formulas); then a light sweep of regular powder to "set" my face. But my eyes are where I really go to town: I dust my bare eyelids with powder to anchor the color, then apply shadow, then powder lightly again. Then I ring them with lotsa liner, followed by mascara. See what I mean? Major maquillage. But somehow, it's not too much.

getting it together
emotionally and spiritually

Now that you've set some important "Mom Matters" precedent after reading Parts 1 and 2 (e.g., building your support network, making time for doctor visits, boosting your energy, and trimming your tummy), it's time in Part 3 to focus on your emotions and spirit. This is the important inner work you'll be doing, from making sure your self-talk is positive to dreaming (dreams are key to recharging emotionally), and possibly learning how to meditate. Even if you don't consider yourself very spiritual, you'll learn lots of ways to reduce that mountain of new-mama stress.

chapter•thirteen

watch your mouth: the importance of positive self-talk

True crunchy-granola story: Recently, after coming home from work and swapping out my slinky dress and slouchy boots for a soft T-shirt and comfy linen "beach pants" from Victoria's Secret (order a pair in every color, now), I was puttering around my office/girl power sanctuary when Hubby popped in to ask me how my day went. "Great," I said. "Every day is a good one when you control your thoughts." "Definitely," replied Hubby.

No, we're not robots. And no, we don't belong to a cult. We're just two people in our mid-to-late forties who have finally—after quite a bit of soul searching—discovered that a big part of happiness and contentment lies not in an external anything, but in the way we structure and maintain our inner dialogue.

So what does this have to do with you, a weary mama bear with barely enough time to catch her breath between nappy changes and feedings? And what's the connection between our thoughts and our "inner dialogue?" In short, everything. Good thoughts generate good feelings, which are typically accompanied by healthy, happy self-talk. And healthy, happy self-talk = a healthier, happier you. In fact, positive self-talk is so vital to your well-being that this just might be the most important chapter in this book.

this is huge

No matter how close you are to the people in your life—and you might feel all but welded to your baby at the moment—the only person who's with you nonstop throughout your entire life is you. That's why it's so crucial that you learn to chat with yourself (and we all chat with ourselves) in a supportive way that allows you to be not only your best self, but completely nice to yourself in the process.

Moms, especially first timers, can find this mental terrain difficult to navigate. With so many opportunities to second guess yourself, it's easy to get into a groove where your self-talk is anything but supportive. "From the moment you give birth, your inner voice—I like to call her 'She'—kicks in," says Jill E., mama of two. "'She' is usually caring and complimentary, but 'She' can question you and rock your security, too. We all want to be Supermom—present, accountable, engaged, taking care of everything and everyone around us—all the while being both patient and kind. That's not always easy."

It's *not* always easy, but if I'm smart I'll take a few minutes first thing in the morning to mentally set the tone for how I want the next eighteen hours to unfold. Because, newsflash, we get to choose that. I can decide to start the day on a defeatist note and let myself be bashed around by all the little stuff (a missed train, a splash of tomato bisque across my crisp white shirt) and heap lots of abuse on myself about being disorganized (totally false) or clumsy (maybe a little). Alternatively, I can choose to recognize how insignificant those petty annoyances are to the overall scheme of things and dial back in to how great my life actually is.

If you're still in the "newborn bubble," much of your own unsupportive self-talk undoubtedly stems from fear. Baby raising can seem so foreign, and it's so much hard work. "With a first child, you're so nervous," says author and Divalysscious Moms founder Lyss Stern, mama of two. "There's a whole 'first-time' psychology happening." No wonder you chew yourself out on occasion; according to the Official New-Mom Handbook in your head, you're not up to snuff, right? Wrong! Trust me, as soon as you learn to prop yourself up with your inner dialogue rather than tear yourself down, the whole "mom thing" gets infinitely easier.

Just ask Elizabeth, mama of two, who has pretty much tamed the negative self-talk beast. "I catch myself doing it now," she says. "Sometimes it's hard to stop, but then I tell myself that I am who I am, that I'm competent, and that I'm trying my hardest." I don't know about you, but "trying my hardest" sounds pretty damn great to me. Clearly, when the going gets a little rough, Elizabeth is making it her business to speak to herself in a loving, constructive manner, and so should you!

postbaby is a prime time for a good talking-to

In Chapter 3 we discussed the issue of sky-high mommy expectations and the psychological trap they can lay for an unsuspecting mama in training. When things don't go exactly as planned, a typical default reaction is to point the finger at yourself. Sailing uncharted baby seas can be tricky, and it's only natural that the chatter inside your head can take a dark turn when you have no clue which way is up.

Melissa, mama of four (yup, you read that right, four), remembers those times well! "I can vividly recall these conversations in my head in which I'd say, 'I have no idea what this little one needs. And I'm so tired I could vomit.'" Melissa remembers an evening when she couldn't get her daughter Bella to sleep for all the tea in China. "I tried everything. My husband, too, but to no avail," she says. "So I decided to take her outside in the stroller at about 11:00 P.M. On my fourth or fifth lap around the block, this kind-hearted man came out of his building and said that he and his wife had had a colicky baby too, that I shouldn't get frustrated, and that I wasn't alone."

That was all Melissa needed to hear. "I can't tell you how encouraging it was to hear his words at that moment. He pulled me out of my own little world and made me realize this was all perfectly normal. I instantly relaxed. Bella did, too, and quickly nodded off. Because of the profound effect this had on me, I will, without hesitation, walk over to a mom in need and reassure her she's not alone, that we've all been there." The 'work,' as they say in therapy, is to convert similar "I can do this" thoughts into your own ongoing interior soundtrack.

When you're in the thick of it, it's hard to believe that your situation will improve, but it always gets better. There aren't too many sure things in this life, but you can pretty much bet that, with time, two miraculous changes will occur in Babyville. One, your DD will just naturally calm down and settle into a nicer groove of eating more and sleeping better. At the same time, you'll gain confidence, so the temptation to be hard on yourself will subside a bit.

directing some of that mama love inward

Before we start to break down our old bad self-talk habits, it's helpful to know how we arrived at them in the first place. According to Itsy Bitsy Yoga founder Helen Garabedian, one big reason our self-talk is less than loving is that we weren't given the tools to switch it up when we were children ourselves. Her theory is that if you're old enough to be reading this book, chances are you weren't taught how to shape your self-talk in a more helpful manner.

"A lot of people aren't used to a positive inner dialogue," says Garabedian. "And you know why? As we were growing up, we didn't hear all the affirmations like that we're smart and creative, that we now know are beneficial. So now that we're parents, we're trying to incorporate those affirmations into our own lives, and into the lives of our children."

In my opinion—and I'm sure I'll hear from the Hubby Police about this—one of the main reasons we mamas are so hard on ourselves is that we naturally assume a care-giving role for everyone in our household. Because of that, we have umpteen more opportunities than our partners do to feel like we didn't quite ace a situation. Toss a still-poochy postpartum belly into the mix and it's a wonder we ever crawl out from underneath the covers.

Join me, please, on the journey to turn it all around. If you want peace of mind and to feel like you're whizzing through your life with more emotional energy and freedom, you have to dig deep, teach yourself the basics of positive self-talk, and then actively, consciously, and rigorously apply that newfound knowledge—even when you feel those evil "bad mommy" thoughts creeping back in. So here goes; here are the easy-to-wrap-your-head-around-but-not-so-easy-to-execute steps to a better inner dialogue.

Step One: Challenge Your Negative Assumptions

A lot of our bad thoughts about ourselves—and the inner dialogue we produce as a result of those bad thoughts—is based on flat-out reality distortion. Fight nonsense with sense. For instance, you may find yourself saying something along these lines: "All the other moms in Gymboree feed their kids homemade organic baby food. I'm not doing all I can do to make sure little Susie gets a healthy head start." If so, follow up immediately with self-talk like this: "Hmmm . . . if that's true, then why hasn't little Susie had so much as a sniffle all winter? And why is she off the growth charts in height and weight?"

Step Two: Replace Them with Something Stronger, Healthier, and Happier.

This step gives you a way to "reframe" your first negative thought/self-talk in a way that benefits both you and your wee one. Using the example above, you could say something like, "Wow, if all these Gymboree moms are feeding their kids homemade organic baby food, maybe it's easier to make than I think it is. I'll check out some recipes online when I get home. It just might be the perfect excuse to get that food processor I've been eyeing at Williams-Sonoma." Now you've spun a potentially unpleasant "bad mommy" thought into one that is so much more positive and constructive. Love it!

practice makes perfect

As you can imagine—or if you can't imagine it yet, I'll just tell you straight up—parenting a child will be chock-full of challenges for at least the next twenty years. It's not as if your cares vanish the second the little darling is potty trained (though that is pretty freaking fantastic). That's why you can never really let up on this positive self-talk stuff; it's just too fundamental to happier parenting and a happier you.

You just need to think of it as building a muscle. You know how sore you were the first time you lifted weights or did ab work postbaby? Each time got a little easier, right? Well, the same thing will happen here if you work hard to keep positive self-talk in your bag of tricks.

For inspiration, I'd like to discuss positive self-talk role models. Trust me, they're out there, mingling among us self-doubters. Though I certainly wasn't one of them, some mothers, for whatever reasons, waddle right out of that labor and delivery ward and seize the day feeling utterly sure of themselves. Others learn on the job, but still manage to keep a lid on their inner critics.

the**mother**load

"I don't know where my mom confidence comes from, but I think I'm a fantastic mother. I often tell my kids that they're so lucky to have me and that I wish I had been my own mom! Maybe it's because my own mother— as funny and loving as she is today—was just so cranky and mean that I wanted to break that cycle. I recall her mothering and I do the opposite. Nothing out of this world, mind you. I just hug my kids. Tell them I love them. Kiss them constantly. Listen to their stories and complaints. Sense their moods. Reprimand them lovingly. Protect their confidence. And tell them they're the best things to have come into my life."

—**Patricia**, mama of twins

Mama of two Gwen is one of these self-talk role models. "I have to say, I've rarely felt bad about myself as a parent," she says. "Don't get me wrong—you feel the responsibility from day one. But I always said that if I could take care of the grownup babies in my office, my own kids should be a piece of cake. When I think of how little our own parents knew—or even wanted to know—about the ins and outs of parenting, that thought gives me a lot of confidence. Because hey, we came out okay."

If you're naturally a little less sure of yourself than the Gwens of the world, don't fret. Just keep repeating those basic steps outlined above and pretty soon you'll be able to take off the training wheels and fly. But leave your helmet on; you never know when you might encounter a pothole on the Road of Life.

when your body chemistry throws you a curve

It completely sucks, but sometimes compromised physical or mental health can make positive self-talk difficult, if not impossible. Whether it's residual baby hormones or a condition predating your DD—such as anxiety or depression—your body chemistry can easily wreak havoc on your sense of well-being.

reserve the right to . . .

. . . consider seeing a therapist if your DIY efforts aren't making a dent in your negative self-talk—even if you've never seen a shrink in your entire prebaby life. Therapy doesn't have to be a lengthy ". . . and then when I was five . . ." type of commitment; certain kinds of counseling, particularly Cognitive Behavioral Therapy, are goal oriented and time efficient. You deserve to learn the proper tools for creating a positive inner dialogue.

Unfortunately, I have firsthand experience with this. Apart from my intermittent anxiety and occasional bouts with cyberchondria, which I've mentioned, my underactive thyroid has also played a role in how I feel about myself. Recently, suspecting that he may need to increase the dosage on the medication I've been taking for the past two years, my internist did blood work. And in between receiving the results of that test and receiving a new, higher-dose prescription, my original Rx ran out and I got caught in a two-week period in which I had no meds.

Because there is a direct corollary between thyroid levels and mood, I wasn't able to fend off bad thoughts with my usual kick-em-to-the-curb force. So not surprisingly, I wasn't a happy camper until my optimal thyroid levels were restored. Nothing drastic happened. I just beat myself up a bit here and there, which I typically don't do anymore.

Only you can be the judge of whether you're feeling less resilient and cheerful than usual. And only you can know what's going on inside your own head. But if you find your self-talk taking a nosedive for no specific reason, see your doctor to determine if there are any underlying medical issues responsible for your low mood.

For any of you battling full-blown anxiety or depression—postpartum or otherwise—know that the last thing in the world you should ever do is try to "talk yourself out of it." Get the medical and psychological help you need, and take comfort in knowing that all of us other mamas are rooting for you.

Now that you're making positive self-talk a round-the-clock habit, what else can you do to manage your myriad new-mama emotions? You might want to try journaling. There are lots of ways to do it, and the benefits are enormous. Read on to find out if journaling is for you.

Adhering to "The Four Agreements"

I don't remember exactly what compelled me to pick up *The Four Agreements: A Practical Guide to Personal Freedom* by Don Miguel Ruiz. But about six months after the DD was born, I decided to give the slim volume a shot. One of the best decisions I've ever made.

Although there's plenty of wisdom in all four of the "agreements" Ruiz urges us to make with ourselves, I've found the second one—"don't take anything personally"—particularly profound. Why? Because for me, much of my negative inner dialogue used to center around what I imagined everyone else was thinking about me. But Ruiz's call to action shows you the futility (not to mention narcissism) of that exercise. Not only is it impossible to know what others are thinking, but even if you did know, there isn't anything you could really do to change it. And here's the kicker: Nine times out of ten, other people aren't even thinking about you anyway. Everyone is so absorbed in his or her own little interior life that they're rarely, if ever, focusing on you.

I'll never forget the first time I embraced this "agreement." I chose a typical workday and promised myself I wouldn't personalize one thing that happened to me. No "living inside my head," no getting huffy and puffy over imaginary transgressions. I just went about my business and was surprised to find I had a lot more energy and focus (of course I did; none of it was being expended trying to read the minds of the people around me.)

That evening, I met one of my besties for a fun dinner. Over yummy pasta, I gushed about my new master plan for lightening up. I couldn't help myself—it was one of the happiest days of my life.

chapter•fourteen

the write stuff

If you've never kept a journal, the idea of starting one right after you've had a baby probably seems like the very definition of insanity. I mean, who has the time, right? Um, you do. And it's a really good idea.

Today, it's widely recognized that journaling can lower your stress levels. And as you'll read in Chapter 15, stress is really, truly the devil's spawn. It makes us sick, makes us sad, and zaps the precious energy we need to care for our tiny tots.

But I'm getting ahead of myself here, because my sole mission right now—to get you in the habit of releasing your thoughts and feelings on a page or computer screen—just might help stop stress from exploding to unmanageable levels in the first place.

processing on paper (or a pc)

It's too late now, but I really wish I'd kept journals more consistently in my many prechild years. Sure, I have snippets; mostly about dating disasters sprinkled with tidbits about my (otherwise fantabulous) social life. But there isn't a real record of all the traveling and footloose and fancy-free fun I had prior to getting landlocked with a baby. When I reread those old scraps, it's alarming to see how worked up I used to get over dudes who didn't wind up being my husband. Even though I could have spared myself some angst, at least I see how focused I was on developing a solid, lasting relationship; and ultimately, I did precisely that. So much so that I now have a charming toddler upstairs chilling in front of the TV watching *Wonder Pets*. And I'm writing a book about the whole thing.

So yes, journals are written time capsules of what we've done, where we've been, and who's zipped in and out of our lives over the years. And for that reason alone, they're worth keeping. It's pretty riveting to go back and read about what you were up to a decade ago, even if (or maybe especially if) you're much happier, productive, and self-constructive today, like I am.

For those of us who are in the midst of a Momover, journaling offers so much more than just a slice of history. In addition to reducing tension—a documented benefit—here are just a few other goodies to be gleaned from putting pen to paper:

- **A private, nonjudgmental space to vent about every-thing**. And maybe that's all you need—a cooling-off zone to get stuff off your chest or a place to stash the mom thoughts you feel guilty about (trust me, every mama has 'em). So consider your journal a written version of a tension-releasing pillow fight.

- **An opportunity to view situations from a 360-degree angle**. Journals provide an opportunity to sift through your feelings about the people, places, and events in your life. Chances are if you take the time to write about and digest a situation, you'll be less likely to engage in a pitched battle. And—gasp—you might even begin to appreciate the other person's perspective.

- **A window into negative patterns**. Over time, you might detect that you snack too much when you're bored, that it's finally time to dump that "frenemy" who always manages to say the wrong thing, or that your partner really needs to help out more around the house. Recognizing what isn't working in your life—whether it's due to your own actions or someone else's—is the first step toward change.

- **A window into positive patterns**. You're bound to have reasons to celebrate, and a journal is a wonderful catch-all for that. Perhaps you're finally in a good place with your mother-in-law, or your toddler's ballet teacher routinely praises her attention and focus. Or maybe you've been extra diligent about exercising or have learned to squelch unproductive self-talk. These are triumphs that deserve to cherished in your diary, even if you're the only one to see them.

- **Intense self-knowledge**. If you commit to total honesty in your journal, you'll really get to know who you are—as a woman and, now, as a mother. And that, my mama friend, is powerful stuff.

it's not about winning a pulitzer

Ironically, professional writers (or at least this professional writer) sometimes have a tough time journaling. Why? Because it's hard to just jot down our thoughts willy-nilly, with little to no attention paid to the "quality" of those words or the way they're structured. But that's exactly what journaling demands—a quickie stream of consciousness that isn't edited down to the last syllable. Thinking too hard defeats the purpose; ditto for revisions. What good is recording your thoughts and feelings if you're just going to come back later and rerecord?

Of course, editing is far easier on a computer, which is another reason for writer types to go the Luddite-ish pen and paper path. So, if you have word-perfection issues, regardless of whether you're a professional writer or not, consider an old-time journal. Besides, it's fun to splurge on a new one. Make it festive and it'll be that much more fun to write in. And then just go for it and spill. Don't worry what it "sounds" like, because you're the only one who's "listening."

reserve the right to . . .

. . . make it all up, by diving into a little fiction writing. Start with a short story, and who knows, you might just wind up penning the next great American novel. Writing fiction can be an amazing respite from stress and a fun way to work out your "issues" anonymously. A mama friend of mine and I have had the best time thrashing out our (still unpublished) chick-lit masterpiece. And remember: You can always keep it all to yourself.

wish lists and other "micro journals"

For any of you who might feel intimidated at the prospect of staring down a blank sheet of paper, know that tiny little tidbits in the form of blue-sky wish lists and paragraph-length "micro journals" can also serve the same purpose—recording your thoughts, feelings, and deepest desires. You can even just e-mail yourself and stuff them into a "journal" file in your computer. My point is this: Feel free to keep it short and simple, sister. I'm actually very fond of wish lists. Here's why.

Several years ago, not long after I'd gotten married, I attended a workshop given by Henriette Anne Klauser, author of *Write It Down, Make It Happen* (details in the Dig Deeper Appendix). A tall, energetic woman with a million stories to tell, Klauser's enthusiasm for attracting good things into your life merely by putting pen to paper was contagious.

At some point in the evening, she asked us to make wish lists of goals or scenarios we'd like to see unfold in our lives in the future. We were then instructed to insert those lists into a self-addressed stamped envelope and fork them over to her. Her intention was to babysit them for a while and then mail them back to us in six months. By then, Klauser promised, a good chunk of those wishes were very likely to have come true. And if they hadn't already, there was a high likelihood that they were at least percolating.

Long story short: While it was fun to see my list surface via snail mail a half-year later, I didn't think much of it because three of my biggest wishes—getting pregnant, moving into a beautiful new home, and writing a book—were nowhere near reality at that point. Years later, of course, those desires came through in spades. And since that time, I've become a wish-list convert. Though it often takes much longer for my dreams to manifest than I'd like, in time, most of them do come to fruition. And you know what? I'll take "eventually" over "never" any day.

Besides wish lists, there are other great approaches to "micro journaling." Garabedian recommends what she calls "intuition journals." By tracking brief flashes of insight by either writing them down or remembering them, Garabedian believes new mothers can learn to trust that they know exactly what they're doing on the baby-raising front. She says, "Three weeks after birth, the mother knows and understands more about her baby than anyone else— including doctors. But what happens is that moms aren't accustomed to paying attention to their intuition, and they should be."

Garabedian says we shouldn't be shy about recording even our smallest hunches. Let's say you're driving past a store and a quart of milk flashes through your mind. If you discover later that you don't have enough milk for a recipe you're making, that's an example of intuition. Or you might just suspect that your tot's cough is serious enough to warrant a trip to the doctor—despite the fact that Hubby feels otherwise. (This is a frequent scenario in my own household, but I prefer to err on the side of caution.) Although getting confirmation from your pediatrician that your baby is indeed ill is never great, over time, all those instances when your intuition is spot-on begin to pile up, and your mom confidence grows by leaps and bounds.

the**mother**load

"When my first child was born I kept details for a year, but it was mostly about his routine. Now I don't keep a journal or a blog, but every year my husband and I try to reflect on the year that has passed and we write a letter to our children, which they can read when they get older. I think I have a lot to say about being a mom, but never thought any-one would be interested in hearing it."

—**Gwen**, mama of two

As I mentioned earlier, another easy way to "go small" when keeping track of your thoughts and activities is to simply e-mail yourself. I sometimes do this when I'm trying to lose weight and want to trace my daily food intake. At work, for instance, I'll send an e-mail home to myself about what I've had for lunch or snacks that day.

So just let go of preconceived notions of what a "journal" is. Your journal is whatever you say it is. Who knows, you might even invent a whole new genre.

blogging rights: going public

Out of curiosity, I recently Googled the word "mom" to see what blogs might crop up. Who knew? There are like ten million. There's even a massive portal called The Mom Blogs (*www.themomblogs .com*), the goal of which is "to create the most comprehensive directory of blogs by moms."

A lot of these blogs are merely written by mothers and have content about a specific hobby (scrapbooking is a big one) or pertain to a certain interest group, such as single mamas or moms of children with disabilities. But some deal specifically with the experience of being a mom, getting into the nitty-gritty of daily life with little Sally Sue or Billy Blue, right down to poopy diapers and projectile vomiting.

Maybe because I'm already living all that (well, not the diapers anymore, hurrah!), I find myself drawn more toward the other kind of mom blog—the ones geared toward hobbies and special interests. Which isn't to say that some of the mom-experience blogs aren't funny, interesting, and witty, because they definitely are.

Surprisingly, though I have a lot of friends who are writers, none of them blog about the ins and outs of raising their tots. "I keep a journal and I recently started a blog, but neither is too devoted to my thoughts on motherhood," says twins mama Patricia. 'Well, maybe the blog a little more so, since I love sharing my kids' sense of humor with the few people who read it. But I'm just not that absorbed by motherhood. Why is that?" Katherine, mama of one, seconds that emotion. "I have all sorts of journals and blogs," she says, "but hardly any are about the experience of being a mom."

If you opt to go the blogging route, just be clear that it isn't journaling. If you're laying it all out there for the world to see, you won't be getting the full benefit of venting privately. For starters, would you really share your deepest thoughts, both positive and negative? Doubtful. So, at least in some small measure, you'll be editing and cleaning it all up for public consumption. Otherwise, it would be a bit like bringing a video camera into a session with your shrink. And you wouldn't do that, would you?

the big picture(s)

If I had to pick one main reason for you to journal, it would be to improve your mental and physical health by providing yourself with a private dumping ground for all of your deepest, darkest thoughts and frustrations about mothering. Get those puppies off your chest and you'll be at least halfway to feeling better. Or in my case, sleeping through the night without waking up and wondering how I'm going to keep so many life balls juggling in the air.

But let's just say you're just not into it. Fair enough. Maybe you'll get there someday, maybe you won't. Still, I encourage you to keep some kind of record of this time, whether it's a scrapbook or one of those first-year journals you were undoubtedly gifted with at your baby shower. Personally, I'm obsessed with the gorgeous picture books you can create yourself on a Mac computer (you can also go online to one of the many picture book-making sites, including *www.ourhubbub.com*, *www.picaboo.com*, and *www.printcreations.com*). My good friend Debi has made really stunning collections of family trips to London, her daughter's bat mitzvah, and summers at the beach, and I'm making a beautiful one of our DD for Hubby's upcoming 50th birthday. However you decide to chronicle your DD's early years, just do it! I don't want you to look back on this monumental time in your own life and not have a way to instantly channel the amazing cocktail of emotions that having a baby stirred up. It's just too damn important.

Now that you're incorporating some form of journaling into your life (or flaunting your inner artist with some drop-dead beautiful picture books of your DD), you'll be thrilled to see what a tension releaser it can be. But for even more—many more, in fact—super-effective ways to defuse new-mama stress, simply read on. The next chapter gives you the full rundown on stress—how it affects us physically and mentally, and how to make it go bye-bye.

Expanding My Self-Care Chart

In the spirit of "walking the talk," I've recently started yet another gut-wrenching, warts-and-all journal. But since my entries are still fairly sporadic, I've decided to continue with my own special mash up of a classic journal and my little home-from-the-hospital self-care chart I told you about in Chapter 1.

I first started my new and improved, expanded self-care chart during my "summer of stress," a gruesome stretch when my DD was about eighteen months old and my health was far from optimal. I was dealing with fatigue (and chubbiness!) related to my underactive thyroid, and the dermatologist had discovered that gnarly precancerous patch of skin on my forehead, putting my anxiety in overdrive. So taking into account my dodgy health and high stress level, here's what my expanded self-care chart was comprised of originally:

- Previous night's sleep
- Weight
- Prescription meds, OTC vitamins, and supplements taken throughout the day
- Exercise
- Relaxation (i.e., aromatherapy bath, half-hour with a good book, mini yoga or meditation session)

And here's what I've gradually added:

- Water intake
- Immunity boosters (dry brushing my skin, wheatgrass juice, etc.)
- Life snapshot (i.e., a brief overview of what's happening, as in "juggling lots of deadlines right now" or "the entire family has the flu" or "looking forward to our long weekend in Montauk")

- How I'm feeling physically on a scale of one to ten, with quick, relevant details (i.e., "peppy because of my morning run")
- How I'm feeling mentally and emotionally on a scale of one to ten, with quick relevant details (e.g., "sad because of whopper argument w/Hubby about where to spend the holidays")

I'll be the first to admit that this isn't the scintillating read, but it at least gives me a ballpark idea of what's going down on Planet Dana. And while I know it's overkill, I still keep a separate fitness log. It lives in my gym bag, so it's always handy for whipping out the second I hop off the elliptical or get back home after a run. In this particular "journal" I don't need to record my feelings, because they're always the same: happy and proud that I'm taking primo care of myself (and trimming my thighs in the process).

chapter•fifteen

stress is worse than a dirty diapee

Okay, so ten months of pregnancy can get a little annoying. Labor and delivery isn't a barrel of laughs, either. But at least those conditions/events have a beginning, middle, and an end. Stress, on the other hand, can be relentless. Unless you take steps to prevent it, it just hangs around, lying in wait.

It would be one thing if stress were merely a huge pain in the ass, but it's actually far more insidious than that. In fact, if it isn't consciously, deliberately released on a regular basis, it can trigger a cascade of ailments ranging from a fairly innocuous case of the sniffles to something more serious, like an ulcer or high blood pressure. Many well-regarded health gurus even believe that a link exists between stress and certain types of cancer. And at the very least, it messes big time with your quality of life. That's the bad news about stress. The good news is that there's plenty you can do about it.

no kidding: postbaby peace of mind ain't easy

Any major life change, even good stuff like getting hitched or moving into the human equivalent of Barbie's Dream House, will upset the emotional and physical applecart. And I'd be hard pressed to find a bigger life change than giving birth—even if you've been hoping, wishing, and praying for it for years before it eventually happens.

For first timers, there's the initial learning curve to get through. Then, once you finally start to get your sea legs, it's still a good solid year before your tot can communicate well enough to let you know something's up. Until then, you have to rely on any number of visual and proto-verbal cues, like a continual tug on a tiny ear to let Mom know an infection is brewing or a sweet little Cro-Magnon grunt to make it clear that mashed peas should be taken off the dinner menu.

Sure, that might not sound like stress. Mothers have been taking care of babies for thousands of years, right? And when you're feeling on top of your game, you might not even realize the subtle, round-the-clock pressure you're under. On other days (the bad ones, the ones that seem to last forty-eight hours instead of twenty-four), you'll know damn well what's going down. Besides, those Zen mamas from thousands of years ago? They might not have had a washer or dryer, but you better believe their lives were a lot less frantic than ours.

Eventually, stress will start to make its presence known physically, in the form of minor symptoms that can, and frequently do, lead to much bigger problems. You might notice that you've been having headaches a little more frequently than you used to or that your annual cold boomerangs back two or three more times before the winter finally drizzles to an end. Before you know it, that lingering fatigue you wrote off as a mere lack of sleep is diagnosed as an underactive thyroid.

the**mother**load

"This is the one area I'm not good at—controlling or managing stress. I try to balance motherhood with work, which sometimes reduces my stress level, but sometimes also contributes to it. I wish I had some words of wisdom to share, but for me, stress is a big part of my day to day. So for now I deal with it, know it's part of my day and my life. And I try in some bigger ways to be sure I take care of myself so that I can relieve stress and rejuvenate in bigger chunks of time."

—Jill E., mama of two

how mental strain makes us sick

Clearly, stress is not fun. But why does it happen?

I could basically answer this question with a single sentence: Stress makes us sick because it weakens our immune systems. But I think you deserve a better, more nuanced explanation, one that, hopefully, motivates you to take the steps necessary to either reduce the amount of stress in your own life or at least consciously mitigate it with relaxation exercises, deep sleep, a sound diet, and other good-for-you lifestyle changes.

Acute Stress

In a nutshell, there are two main types of stress: acute and chronic. Acute stress generates a stop-you-in-your-tracks feeling, the way you feel when something unexpected and awful happens, such as a car accident or a suggestion by your doctor that a biopsy is done on some suspicious-looking patch on your boob or belly. Parenting is also fraught with these quick, painful "bad-mommy" jabs, such as when your toddler falls off a stool and bangs his precious little head.

However, as I mentioned earlier, short-lived stress can also crop up when something wonderful transpires, like getting engaged. I remember feeling anxious after Hubby proposed, and I was forty! I guess after so many years as a reluctant bachelorette, it seemed surreal that that era was finally, happily drawing to a close. Your baby's first steps might be another example of acute stress. That's because you're simultaneously filled with pride and terrified your little miss or mister is about to take a nosedive into the coffee table.

So that's acute stress, which subsides quickly and usually doesn't leave a trail of trouble in its wake. Unless it's the really ramped-up version—post-traumatic stress disorder—which I'll circle back around to later.

Chronic Stress

Chronic stress, brought on by, say, toxic office politics or caring for a sick loved one, is the bad guy. This is the kind of stress that gradually takes a mental and physical toll. And it also ages us prematurely, which is highly undesirable for hot mama bears like you. I'm not saying that acute stress isn't bad, but because it subsides quickly it doesn't chip away at your health and immune system to the same degree that chronic stress does.

Actually, it's the byproduct of stress—the release of hormones such as adrenaline and cortisol—that can cause the real problems, says Dr. Jill Baron, a New York-based family practitioner who specializes in integrative medicine and frequently counsels her patients in stress-management techniques. (To learn more, visit her website at *www.dontmesswithstress.com*.) Because we almost never actually use these hormones for anything (they're a biological holdover from the saber-tooth tiger and woolly mammoth era), they just build up in our bodies, wreaking havoc. "The 'fight-or-flight' response evolved, in primitive times, for when people encountered lions," says Dr. Baron. "These days, let's say you see a mugger coming toward you—the same response occurs. If you perceive a threat, even if it's only in your mind, you can start getting anxious or fearful, and hormones get released."

In turn, these hormones divert blood to your major muscle groups, like your legs (so you can make a speedy getaway); they make your pupils dilate (so you can see exactly what's going on); and they break down your sugar and fat stores (so you have the energy to engage in a fierce battle with the enemy).

Unfortunately, because of the crazed, nonstop lives we lead these days, we can become so permanently wired and tense that we have a hard time distinguishing between real and imaginary threats. And if we're really on edge, we'll hurl a saber tooth tiger-level reaction at a minor annoyance. "If you're standing in the ten-item Express Lane and the person in front of you has twenty-five items, the smoke is coming out of your ears," says Dr. Baron, describing a typical over-reaction scenario. "So hormones are being produced, they're circulating in your body, but you're not burning them up. That's very harmful." For instance, as a type-A New Yorker, I can get extremely hyped up when anything messes with my full-steam-ahead routine, such as someone snatching a taxi out from under my nose. But all those small bursts of fury get me is a wave of hormones circulating in my body that don't really have a way to burn themselves out.

And that's not good, because too much stress-hormone buildup without release can result in suppression of the immune system. And we all know what happens when our immune systems are flying at half-mast: illness. So do yourself a favor and don't underestimate the strain you're under. "New moms probably have a low level of stress hormones just kind of simmering in the background," says Dr. Baron. "That's why it's really important to have coping strategies."

just say no to going ballistic

It's important to remember that stress means different things to different mamas. For instance, if you tend to be obsessive-compulsive about your daily to-do list, not making one will freak you out even more than making one, even if it's a mile longer than it used to be prebaby. In fact, ticking off a bunch of back-burnered chores—what doctor-authors Michael F. Roizen and Mehmet C. Oz call NUTs (Nagging Unfinished Tasks)—can feel pretty awesome. Read more about NUTs in Roizen and Oz's book *You Staying Young: The Owner's Manual for Extending Your Warranty*, listed in the Dig Deeper Appendix.

Whether large or small, we all have our own personal can of NUTs. Right now, I'm thinking of the stack of sweaters in my closet that need hand washing. By the time I get around to dousing them in Woolite, it will be time to pack them away for the season. But guess what? Whenever I finally do tackle that task, I'll be psyched. I'm a big old weirdo, but I utterly love doing little chores like that.

reserve the right to . . .

. . . exchange freaked-out, "I'm losing it" phone calls with a like-minded mama friend. You can schedule them (á la every Tuesday night at 9:00 P.M.) or make an agreement that each of you gets one a week (or more, if necessary). The only rule is that the "receiving mama" has to stop what she's doing for five or ten minutes and really listen. Aaaah . . . instant stress relief.

Whether it's small and NUT-like or a larger life issue that's caus-ing you agita, the following list of fast, effective techniques can work for any mama and any meltdown.

- **Consciously "reframe" the situation to dial back the ten-sion.** This is a perfect chance to use those self-talk skills we discussed in Chapter 13. For example, rather than flipping out over the fact that your wee one just hurled her bowl of oatmeal across the kitchen, take the emotion out of the equa-tion in a mellow, detached, "Hmmm, better grab the paper towels" manner. (I reframe constantly; once you give it a try, it's pretty addictive.)

- **Take a deep breath (or six).** So basic. So completely spot-on.

- **Snap on the baby carrier and take a walk around the block.** You'll burn off stress and a handful of calories at the same time.

- **Pick up the phone or fire off an e-mail to a friend.** Isola-tion is stressful, and if it's just you and the baby for most of the day, there's a good chance you feel cut off from the rest of humanity.

- **Kick off your shoes and do a little reflexology.** This ancient natural therapy, which is based on the theory that particular reflexes in the feet are connected to every other body part, is widely considered to promote relaxation and deeper sleep. There's even a portable iPhone app for this now! Learn more at the extremely comprehensive *www.reflexology-research.com*.

- **Imagine your baby thanking you.** This adorable tip, courtesy of Itsy Bitsy Yoga founder Helen Garabedian, is a powerful antidote for those overwhelmed and resentful feelings that can crop up in caring for a newborn. "When you're in the middle of a stressful moment, think about what your baby wants to appreciate you for," Garabedian advises.

"Our babies don't have words, but if they did, they would love to say so many sweet things. So as you gaze at your baby, recognize what they're showing you. Take every kind of care-giving task and use it as an opportunity to feel their appreciation." Don't you love that? I'm feeling calmer just writing this.

long-term stress busters

There are four key pillars of long-term stress reduction, so think of them as the legs of one of those bar stools your behind was glued to back in your prebaby single days. They are, in no particular order:

- Exercise
- Sound nutrition
- Deep sleep
- Focused relaxation techniques (i.e., yoga and meditation)

There's other stuff that can be helpful over the long haul, too, like positive self-talk. But hopefully I've already convinced you of the importance of engaging in that kind of supportive inner dialogue. So for now, let's heap some major love on "the big four."

Each of these pieces of the health puzzle is so important that they warrant their own separate chapters in this book. So with the exception of calming foods, which I discuss below, I won't delve too deeply here. But I do think it's interesting to note the stress-relieving commonalities woven through these four pillars. Either a few or all of them can lower our heart rates, boost our immunity, produce focused energy, and release "happy" hormones like endorphins and serotonin while short circuiting the bad guys like cortisol and epinephrine.

So educate yourself and clear the decks for eating and sleeping well, working out, and practicing some form of purposeful relaxation. By making it your mission to incorporate these four long-term stress busters into your stay-healthy strategy, you'll feel like you can handle just about anything life tosses your way.

the food-serenity connection

Although it almost always backfires, we sometimes use sweet treats to try to hop us up. You know, the morning Krispy Kreme or the 4:00 p.m. Twix bar approach to energy and vitality. But know this: sugar is a vampire. It depletes you physically and it depletes you mentally. It's even been described as cancer's best friend, which ought to tell you something. So please, please keep your sugar consumption to a dull roar. Instead, reach for foods that calm you. The goal is slowly released, sustainable energy, not the hyper kind that results from a short-lived sugar rush.

In her insanely detailed book *Food & Mood: The Complete Guide to Eating Well and Feeling Your Best,* author Elizabeth Somer connects the dots between the myriad ways our nutrition affects our stress level, and vice versa. Since stress is pretty much unavoidable, especially for new mamas, isn't it kind of great to know that you can reduce some of it (or at least keep it from getting worse), with what you eat and drink all day? I certainly think so!

While I recommend nabbing a copy of this fascinating book (details in the Dig Deeper Appendix), I want to give you a cheat sheet on some of the guidelines that Somers recommends when you hit a rough patch:

- It's natural to crave sweets and crummy white-flour carbs when you're stressed, but giving into those cravings is probably the worst thing you can do. There are about a million healthier alternatives, from fresh fruit to fig bars, so have at them.

- Booze, colas, coffee, and high-fat foods should also be avoided like the plague, at least until your moody storm clouds lift. Instead, consider dabbling in a low-fat vegetarian diet and drinking Teecinno instead of coffee.
- Increasing your intake of B vitamins will help shore up your body's defenses. In Chapter 1, I listed several foods that have a calming effect, some of which will be repeated here. According to Somers, great sources of B vitamins are dark-green leafy veggies, baked potatoes, avocadoes, bananas, fish, and chicken without the skin—remember, skin has fat, and fat increases stress hormones.

It may take some time before you automatically connect the dots between your diet and how you feel, but I promise that it gets easier. And it's great to know how much nutritional control you have over the way you feel.

to each her own destressing

While developing good stress-busting habits is crucial, you'll never be able to obliterate all of the pressure that comes from living in this wacky world of ours. And even attempting to do so or worrying about the way you comport yourself around your child in tense moments can completely exacerbate the problem.

"The most frustrating aspect of having kids is that you can't totally be yourself," says Patricia, mama of two. "You can't fully react to a stressful situation in a way that you used to. If you have a fight with your husband, you can't yell as loudly as you want because that will scare them. If you're sad, you can't crawl into a dark room to cry because that will freak them out, too. I'm sure that leads to a repression of feelings that is ultimately more stressful. However, since I'm clear on that, I do yell a little and I do cry a little. I've explained to my children that life isn't always fun, that I'm human, and that that's just how things go."

I, like Patricia, say go ahead and vent on occasion. You'll know when your stress is rising to an unhealthy level, and you can take the steps you need to get it back under control. I have faith in you—and so should you. Peace out, mama, and remember to have some fun while you're at it!

worked for me!

Targeted Nutritional Supplements

Ever have a day that's just wall-to-wall drama? For me, one such twenty-four hours unfolded when my wee one was about eighteen months old. That was the morning that my derm informed me that there was a high likelihood that the flaky patch on my forehead I assumed was eczema was probably a precursor to skin cancer. Later that day, after literally having electrodes attached to my skull in the New York offices of brain guru Eric Braverman, MD, I was promptly pronounced to be a mess. "You need Xanax," Dr. Braverman said.

Maybe I did, but any time my comes-and-goes anxiety gets to the point that I start considering prescription meds, I take a harder look at my life instead. Usually, there's something I can fix, like leaving a job or a relationship that just isn't working for me anymore. This time, however, I couldn't just cut and run. What was I gonna do? Hand the DD over to Hubby and say, "See ya"?

So, instead of filling the antianxiety Rx that Dr. Braverman wrote for me, I decided to try two of his nutritional supplements. I took (and still take) Brain Energy during the day and Brain Calm before bedtime. And I have to say the difference has been profound. Not long after I started taking them, it dawned on me that I'd probably been suffering from low-grade postpartum depression, which may have been triggered by my traumatic postdelivery blood transfusion. Throw a low thyroid into the mix and it's no wonder I was having a hard time greeting my days with a smile.

I won't try to explain why Dr. Braverman's Brain formulas have worked so well for me. Apparently, it has to do with the replenishment of a few "neurotransmitters" I was missing. (If you'd like to learn more about his work, read his amazing book *The Edge Effect: Achieve Total Health and Longevity With the Balanced Brain Advantage*.) All I know is that I feel really good: relaxed, happy, productive, and Xanax free.

chapter•sixteen

time-outs aren't just for tykes

Fun. You remember that, right? Just like sex, it's that stuff you used to have at the drop of a hat before your little lovey arrived.

Prebaby—minus all the hours I logged at the office, of course—I had so much "me time" it was ridiculous. That's what happens when you don't become a mom until you're forty-three. There were multiple trips to Paris, endless afternoons spent drifting through museums and power shopping, weekends at the beach. And then, with the arrival of you-know-who, all that dreamy leisure activity went up in a puff of smoke.

It happens to every mama bear. And guess what; you mourn the loss of your precious freedom for a spell and then you start getting creative. Maybe you can't get away for the weekend, but you can certainly hide out in a walk-in closet with a video iPod and a box of bon-bons. If anyone needs a break, it's you. So squeeze some fun into your long, taxing days. Who needs moping around?

the perfect ten

As mama of two and founder of Divalysscious Moms, Lyss Stern is an expert at mommy time-outs. And that's why her book, *If You Give a Mom a Martini: 100 Ways to Find 10 Blissful Minutes for Yourself*, is so genius. Coauthored with Julie Klappas (also a mama of two), it really nails the notion that taking tiny breaks from all the mothering and family hubbub is the key to staying sane. "We're saying to moms, 'These are some fun things that you can really do,'" says Stern. "And there are lots of things you can do that don't even cost money."

Like, for instance, weeding out your undie drawer and tossing all the monster Grandmama panties you accumulated during your pregnancy. For a neat freak like yours truly, until I can hop back on a plane to Paris, sifting and sorting is my idea of a good time. And Stern is right there with me on this. "I love organizing," she says. "So for me, it felt really good to just clear out my panty drawer. I purged the old stuff and then bought all new, cute underwear." I guess, theoretically, you could break that undie-drawer cleanup into two mommy time-outs: Part 1, Purging; Part 2, Splurging. See how easy this is?

The idea is to get joyful, to trick yourself into thinking that ten minutes (or twenty or thirty—just not the weekends and vacations you had at your disposal prebaby) is a sufficient amount of time to recharge your batteries. If you're organized and recognize "you time" as the priority it totally is, you can probably sneak in two or three time-outs every day. Yup, even when—especially when—you're freaking out or climbing the walls with boredom.

chick lit, trash tv, surfing, and shopping

Besides the fact that they definitely don't involve a DustBuster, there aren't really any firm ground rules for mommy mini breaks. If you're still in the newborn phase and on high alert for every whimper from the nursery, you'll need to line up activities that can quickly take you in and out of "mama head." In other words, it probably isn't a good idea to listen to a self-hypnosis CD or start cooking an elaborate meal involving a stovetop full of percolating pots and pans. Even if those things relax you, you undoubtedly need a bigger chunk of time to execute them well. But once your precious bambina or bambino starts sleeping for longer stretches, the sky's the limit. (Okay, not really, but don't you just love the sound of that?)

Although every mama's notion of a mini break is slightly different, my informal polling tells me that most of them can be divided into a few broad categories: stuff we read (virtually every issue of *Us Weekly*, foodie websites, and lots of frou-frou chick books); stuff we watch (reality TV, "Oprah," and beaucoup Lifetime); and stuff we splurge on (shoes, shoes, shoes, clothes, more shoes).

For example, twins mama Patricia—like me—regularly tunes in to "American Idol." "Television is wonderfully rejuvenating," she says. "I don't watch too much, though. I'd rather buy a crisp new magazine and flip through that on a Saturday morning as I drink my coffee. I also love my commute to work. I know that sounds crazy, but those forty-five minutes of reading or listening to music while staring out the window are priceless."

the**mother**load

"We have to take care of ourselves first and foremost so we can always give our most and do our best. Mom cannot be lowest 'man' on the totem pole all the time, or no one wins! I'm a big believer that a happy, healthy woman is a better mother, so time-outs are an area in which I excel. My indulgences range from little stuff to gigantic splurges, but they're all important."

—**Jill E.**, mama of two

Ditto on the commuting bliss. Since Hubby pried me out of Manhattan and I added a whole extra ten minutes to my daily back-and-forth to work, I've somehow plowed through an insane number of books. And it's not all chick stuff, either; I've been reading a lot of memoirs. I've also developed a fondness for what I call "Tudor porn," meaning basically everything by Philippa "*The Other Boleyn Girl*" Gregory. I find that entire genre—I guess it's technically historical fiction—frisky, fun, and semienlightening. You get a blast from the past mixed in with all the bodice ripping.

Along the same lines are all those new follow-ups to famous literature, like *Mr. Darcy's Diary* or *Letters from Pemberley*. Anyone who has swooned over Colin Firth in the A&E adaptation of *Pride and Prejudice* will surely love this make-believe fluff. And if you've already read all the Austen you can get your mitts on, as I have, it's a way to get your fix without your mind turning to utter mommy mush.

Of course, if you have the energy and focus to tackle self-improvement during your precious time-outs, by all means, do so—but it has to be fun. For example, I bought those Rosetta Stone CDs in the hopes of improving my French. Have I cracked them open yet? No, but I will. And if they don't float my boat, I'll ship 'em right off to Hobby Siberia.

happy half-hour

Our babies aren't the only ones hitting the bottle. Show me a new mama (at least the ones I know), and I'll show you a cocktail shaker in heavy rotation. Kicking back with a little alcoholic bevvie is a big way many new mothers mitigate some of the stress of caring for their wee ones. "I think drinking wine is a right of passage for all new mothers," says twins mama Jenny R. "We're always looking for an excuse to open up a bottle."

From her perch on the west coast, fellow twins mama Christine has concocted the most delicious-sounding cocktail ever. "My stress level has always been pretty high, but it has peaked even more postbabies," she says. "For the first few postnursing months, I made a weak whiskey sour every single night! It was this amazing ritual. I'd go outside, pick a lemon, pick a lime, squeeze them into a glass with ice and simple syrup and then put a half-shot of Jack Daniels in there. It was unbelievably good and a nice dose of vitamin C. I found that it cleared my head and signified the end of the 'mommy' portion of my day. Whatever damage I did to my liver, I'm convinced I made up for in the mental-health department. It also helped me get to bed early for some much-needed sleep."

Personally, I've become a real lightweight on the booze front, so unless I'm going out to dinner, I usually don't imbibe on school nights. But on my weekend dates with Hubby, I'm all about a glass or two of Champs.

Just remember that although booze will absolutely help you fall asleep more quickly, it also messes with your REM sleep. That's your dream state, and you'll learn more about it in Chapter 18.

nipping off to salons and day spa-aaaaaahs

New York women are known for our power grooming, so I guess, for us, a lot of what other gals might consider a treat we just think of as basic beauty maintenance. I'm talking manis/pedis, professional eyebrow plucking, cut, color, blowouts, etc. I've mentioned before that under no circumstances do I miss my standing monthly salon appointment. I even waddled in there aching from my C-section. The way I see it, that scar's under wraps. But my roots—those are front and center.

Still, I really love my salon treks. So yes, I have to go, but I also want to go. And I think that the postbaby period is an excellent time to reassess just how much you really like the salons and day spas you go to on a regular basis. (If you're not already going regularly, postbaby is a primo time to add a salon or day spa to your special-treat bag of tricks.) When time to yourself is at a premium, be sure to make it count.

reserve the right to . . .

. . . set aside a chunk of the family budget for your mommy time-outs—at least for that crucial first year. Maybe it will mean fewer restaurant meals or putting that new washing machine on temporary hold. But what you'll gain in terms of your sanity and sense of well-being will pay you back ten-fold.

So cuts, color, manis—for a lot of moms, those are the musts. But what about the lusts? What about the treatments that don't yield any visible-to-the-public results, like a salt scrub or a Swedish massage? Don't you dare cross them off your time-out to-do list just because there's a new DD on the scene. Maybe they'll shift from the "regular" to the "occasional" column, but there's no reason why they should drop off the menu altogether.

"When you're a new mom, more than ever it's crucial to get a little head space," says Tanya Mackay, the marketing whiz behind Mama Mio skincare and a mother of two. "Mentally, for rest, rejuvenation, and a bit of perspective. And physically, to help ease your body back to reality. All the changes in size and girth mean your body is certainly a foreign country."

Because Mackay and her two business partners are all mamas, they not only have firsthand knowledge of what types of crèmes, scrubs, and lotion do a postbaby body good, they also knew exactly what their pregnancy and postpartum spa treatments should entail. Along with being super-nurturing, their key element is acceptance.

When you're feeling as big as a house and incredibly squishy all over, accepting yourself lock, stock, and barrel isn't easy, but it can be done. Just jump in there with some cheery self-talk. "For us, the whole goal in looking gorgeous is feeling confident," says Mackay. "So when you do take the plunge and go in for a spa day, be sure to pack the right attitude. Shed any negative thoughts and bad-body image clouds and walk in there thinking, 'I have just made a miraculous baby. I'm going to give myself the space and time to get back in touch with myself and my body.'" Be forewarned: both the chipper, life-affirming self-talk and the spa days can be addictive.

get outta town

Attention, newborn mommies: I know it's hard to wrap your hyper-engaged little noggin around this notion, but there will come a time when you will actually be willing to leave your baby. Overnight.

Granted, it took me three years to pull this off, but it wasn't for lack of trying. For whatever reasons, I was up for splitting town sans bébé way before Hubby was. "We should go away by ourselves," I started saying around the time of the tot's first birthday. "Why would we ever do that?" he'd ask in return, genuinely perplexed that I would even put an idea like that on the table. Ouch. But I persevered, and guess what? We've recently had two brief getaways, both involving planes. And I have to say, even getting through the security line at the airport was fun without the little lady and all that godforsaken gear. Of course, we missed her like crazy. So much so that we replayed a cell phone voicemail she left us (with help, naturally; she's not that advanced) about a trillion times. But it was great to have some uninterrupted couple time and to do what we wanted, when we wanted.

By the way, feel free to skip off all by your lonesome. "Twice a year, I take a really extravagant 'mom-cation' totally alone, to We Care spa in Palm Desert," says mama of two Jill E. "Two nights and three days of deep breathing, yoga, massages, colonics, a full range of healers, and juice-bar detoxes. It cleanses both body and soul and I come home feeling re-energized, stress free, totally rejuvenated, and ready to take on any toddler singlehandedly."

Of course, I realize that your baby is your world, but he can't be your everything all the time. So watch a little trashy TV, get away on vacation, and take some time to practice meditation and yoga (you'll learn some easy ways to do that in the next chapter.) After all, recharging your batteries is what your Momover is all about!

worked for me!

Dry Brushing My Skin

If this didn't feel so damn good, I'd never include it in a chapter on self-indulgence. But you'll just have to go with me on this: It's divine.

You spa fanatics are already familiar with having an esthetician take a stiff, bone-dry brush to your bone-dry body to prep the skin for treatments like a head-to-toe salt scrub. For those who've never experienced it before, dry brushing can feel weird at first. But in addition to dislodging flaky skin, it's also super healthy for you.

In a nutshell, dry brushing boosts immunity because it stimulates the circulation of lymph fluid in the body. The lymphatic system ranks right up there with the circulatory system in terms of importance. Basically, this vast network of tiny vessels functions as the septic tank of the body, whisking toxic material from tissue fluids to the lymph nodes, which further pummel the bad guys and prevent any undesirables, including bacteria, from entering the bloodstream. It's a massive job. And in this polluted, stressful world we live in, it's easy for your lymphatic system to become overwhelmed and sluggish.

After my skin-cancer scare, I decided to send my beleaguered epidermis some TLC, and dry brushing was a great way to do it. Although it's often recommended that dry brushing be done right before a shower because of the flaky skin it loosens, I prefer to do it at night, as part of my prebed ritual. And while you can find elaborate directions on the Internet, I don't kick up a big old fuss about it. Using a long-handled brush I got at Whole Foods, I just start with my feet and work my way north toward my heart before moving on to my belly, arms, and back. I love the pink glow it gives me as well as the feeling I've done something good for myself.

How else do I keep the lymph moving? Well, with semiannual lymph-drainage massage at the spa, daily deep-breathing exercises, and rebounding on one of those cute little mini trampolines I mentioned back in Chapter 9. Twenty minutes bouncing around while I'm watching a bit of Matt Lauer, and I've done my morning bit for a healthier lymphatic system.

the om stretch

I now cordially invite you to hop off the hamster wheel, check out of the rat race, and embrace all those other weird rodent analogies for slowing down and tuning into your spirituality.

By this point, you've (hopefully) built yourself a toolkit of quick-fix and long-term tension zappers. Now it's time to raise your stress-management game with yoga and meditation—two sides of the same Zen coin. If you're already into yoga and meditation, that's fantastic. Just keep them on the top of your new-mama priority list and feel free to skip this chapter and slip right into Warrior Pose or a meditative state.

If you're not already a devotee, I want you to know two things right up front: Both yoga and meditation are easy to dive into, and both yield tremendous spiritual, mental, and physical benefits. And guess who else gets a lift when you hit the yoga mat or meditation rug on a regular basis? Your DD, especially if she is still a newborn. "The more Mom relaxes, the more Baby relaxes," says Itsy Bitsy Yoga's Garabedian. "That happens because the baby's autonomic system is still connected to the mother. In other words, the baby's rhythms are still reliant on the mom's rhythms, even after birth. So it's really important for mothers to stay in touch with the way they're feeling."

Along with journaling, yoga and meditation provide an excellent way to access all the changes you have recently gone through. Even if you're a complete newbie (I was myself until quite recently), there's no reason to hold off on dabbling in a little yoga and meditation. After all, anything that helps you, a super-busy new mom, handle all the changes and plot twists your postbaby life has been throwing at you lately is good, good, good. So grab your mat and keep reading.

advanced r&r: yoga

Speaking of twists, if you've ever seen someone turn themselves into a human pretzel in yoga class, you're probably wondering why I'd label this ancient discipline "advanced R&R." Without a doubt, with some of the more vigorous types of yoga, like Kripalu or Bikram, it's possible to get a hell of a workout. In fact, it can be intimidating to try to envision yourself busting out all those moves. But there's also something profoundly relaxing about yoga. Until recently, I'd only attended a handful of classes—maybe ten over the last fifteen years. My official stance on the topic was always, "I only have so many hours a week to devote to exercise, so those really have to count." I wanted to feel that I'd actually done something, not just rolled around on a sticky mat while hardly breaking a sweat.

Now that I'm postbaby (and older and wiser), I crave all that purposeful stretching, the hush-hush environment, the focus on breath and stillness. So I'm stirring yoga into my healthy-body mix, alongside running, jumping rope, and lifting weights. Here I've outlined a few reasons why I think you should consider adding yoga to your own wellness agenda:

Yoga increases . . .

- **Flexibility:** By stretching both major muscles and soft tissue, yoga not only boosts your range of motion, it also makes you less prone to injury as you're flying through your jam-packed days. And who has time to be sidelined with a sprained ankle? Flexibility also has its advantages for shrimps like me. Reaching for that crystal Champs flute on the third shelf of the kitchen cabinet just got a whole lot easier.
- **Upper-body strength:** When you're lifting and lugging your tot and all that gear night and day, strong arms and shoulders are key. Several poses sculpt and shape this area, including Plank, Mountain Fold, and Downward Dog. Bonus: According to yogic principles, this zone encompasses the fourth—or heart—chakra. By building strength here, you're increasing your capacity to give and receive blessings. Nice, huh?
- **Lung capacity:** A recent study out of Thailand indicates that yoga has the ability to boost your lung function by expanding the chest wall via the deep breathing that accompanies poses.

And it makes perfect sense, doesn't it? Because it's so relaxing, yoga allows us to inhale deeply.

And yoga decreases . . .

- **Stress:** Because the ultimate goal of yoga is peace of mind, everything about it is geared toward deep-sixing stress. Along with the deep yogic breathing, the meditation component also ratchets down tension. Though you might not slip into a full meditative state (at least not to the extent you would curled up at home for thirty minutes), while you're perform- ing relaxation postures like Corpse at the end of class, you'll be instructed to focus your thoughts. And focused thoughts = reduced stress.
- **Blood pressure and risk of heart disease:** I'm cheating a bit with this, because yoga has to be coupled with meditation to yield these results. But since this chapter is a combo plate, I figured I'd put it out there. According to research by the Yale School of Medicine, yoga and meditation, when practiced three times per week, can lower your blood pressure and risk of heart disease. Reducing your stress level paves the way for better func- tioning of your blood vessels, specifically the way they expand, contract, and push your blood where it needs to go.

Go for it. You have nothing to lose (except, oh, stress and health risks!) and everything to gain—namely a chill new lease on life.

Yo Mama, Stay Safe

Seasoned yogi mommies may instinctively know how to guard against injury once they head back to class, but for new mamas who are dipping their toes into yoga for the very first time, I wanted to provide plenty of safety tips. And to do that, I turned to Casey Soer, co-owner and cocreator of Spynga (*www.spynga.com*), an innova- tive discipline that marries spinning with yoga. Genius, right?

A new mom herself, Soer knows the ins and outs of the post-partum body and puts her knowledge into practice in her classes. She suggests that new mothers approach the class with a positive mindset, that they use plenty of props to execute the poses more easily, including blocks, a strap, and a blanket, and that they avoid strenuous poses—particularly backbends—altogether until they're fully back to their prebaby selves. Soer says, "At the beginning of each class, I always request that the new mamas in the room be extra kind to themselves. They've just rented out their bodies for the last ten months, and it takes some time to move back in."

As a new mom myself, I certainly wasn't shy about loading up with extra blankets at the beginning of class, which I used liberally to cushion whatever postpartum body part felt a little tender that day. And I also spent a little time on my own practicing a few "classics" such as the sun salutation, a multistep move that starts and finishes with a standing pose and incorporates other basic postures such as Plank and Cobra.

reserve the right to . . .

. . . create your own spiritual mashup, incorporating bits and pieces of yoga, meditation, chanting, prayer, and whatever else lifts you up. The goal is to consciously free yourself from the minutia of daily life. How you achieve that is entirely up to you.

"For sun salutations, I offer modifications that allow students to flow but also take care of their bodies while building their strength back up," says Soer. "For specific standing and seated postures, I promote the use of a strap and/or blocks, and have students bend their knees to release strain on their lower backs. Their abdominal muscles have just been through a fierce journey and need to be built back up again. For hip-opening poses, the use of blocks or blankets underneath the sit bones will help support the spine. It's these subtle modifications that can help us gracefully return to our bodies and truly feel like the beautiful goddess warriors we all are." While I've never thought of myself as "goddess warrior," it sounds pretty great. Maybe I'll even have T-shirts printed up!

We're covering so much ground in this book that there isn't room for a comprehensive primer on yoga. So in the interest of getting you going as quickly as possible, I asked my friend Sari Nisker, co-owner and cocreator of Spynga, for her best advice for newbies.

She recommends that you find a beginner's class and commit to at least a class a week for a minimum of four weeks. While that might seem like a major chunk of time, it goes by in a flash (take my word on this, pretty please), and it will give you an excellent overview of the many benefits of yoga as well as a core understanding of the physical practice. And in a class setting you've got the instructor at your beck and call to explain postures, breathing, meditation, and history. "Many instructors weave stories and metaphors into the sequencing of the class," explains Nisker, "which provide different perspectives and deeper understanding of what this 'yoga stuff' all means."

Once you get a grounding in yoga, you can supplement your practice by using DVDs at home, (Nisker provided her favorites for the Dig Deeper Appendix), but until then, don't be shy about signing up for that beginner's class. You just might make a few like-minded mama friends.

tapping meditation to tame your restless mind

I can't tell you how long "Learn to Meditate" has been sitting on my life-goals list. Not on my ho-hum to-do list, next to "schedule teethcleaning" or "buy Huggies Pull-Ups." I'm talking about the biggie, the list that serves as the repository for my deepest desires for myself, like "Find Hubby" and "Have Baby." That's how important I consider meditation to my overall health and wellness.

So if it's so important, why haven't I tackled it before now? I guess I wasn't ready. Though I'm sure I could've benefited from meditation at earlier stages of my life, I was just too antsy to explore it (and yes, I see the irony in that). Another big reason is that I'd always assumed meditation required a lot of skill and knowledge. Not so. As it turns out, meditation is just like so many other things in life. Sometimes you just have to wade into the shallow end and start splashing around. "There's no 'right' or 'wrong' with meditation," says intuitive guru Michele Bernhardt, a multitasking healer, astrologer, and metaphysician who's produced several guided meditation CDs. (Learn more at her brilliant website, *www.myinnerworld.com*.) "A big part of meditation is your intention."

So at least intend to give meditation a shot, and in the process, you'll be giving yourself the opportunity to relax, gain mental clarity, and connect with your spirituality.

Go with the Flow

As I said, I hope you don't take a page out of my book by contemplating meditation for a good ten years before actually trying it. To help you move your intention into reality and make the whole shebang that much more compelling, here's a list of tips:

- **Designate a sacred space:** For me, it's my walk-in closet. I love the girl-power vibe—the shoes, the dresses, the purses. Attached to my office, my walk-in is a key part of my "Dana Zone." I've stocked it with a few small pillows and a beautiful meditation mat Bernhardt gave me years ago. In one of my shoe cubbies, I've stashed a gorgeous sand timer, pictures of the ocean, candles, meditation CDs, and a player. Though pillows and candles are the norm, trick out your own sacred space with treasures that speak to you.
- **Create a ritual:** This can involve repeating a mantra, listening to particular music (I like Gregorian chants, but you might prefer wind chimes, Tibetan bells, etc.), or inhaling certain

scents. "I think, deep inside, most of us love a ritual," says Bernhardt. "So use sounds, a candle, or some kind of scent—like incense or myrrh. Patchouli is also perfect. With a scent, right away your body says, 'Okay, I'm ready.'"

- **Make sure you're comfy:** Sorry, that means no Spanx. (Kidding. Sort of.) If you're not keen on sitting on the floor with your back erect and your hands on your knees, you can sit in a chair. Just make sure you're maintaining good posture, that you're positioned a few inches away from the back of the chair, and that your feet are on the floor. Kneeling is another possibility, though you might want to use a pillow for support.

- **Observe your thoughts without "feeding" them:** We discuss how tricky this is below, but it becomes easier once you realize that it's all about detachment. For instance, if, midmeditation, you think about the fact that you need to take your DD to the doc, you say to yourself, "I'm having a thought about needing to take the baby to the pediatrician." What you don't do is take that original thought to the next level, as in, "Next Tuesday afternoon might work" or "I hope the poor little doll doesn't need too many shots." Just let those snippets pass in and out without reaction.

the**mother**load

"I've gotten much more deeply spiritual since I had my child. I trace it directly to being pregnant with him. I was introduced to the notion that our babies choose us as parents. Well, that terrified me to my core. So, I started an intense inner dialogue with my unborn child about who I really am, what kind of mother I hoped to be, my hopes and dreams, etc. To do that, I had to really dig deep and explore the whole 'Who Am I? Why Am I Here?' business. It got me on the path that has led to my becoming a meditation coach. I meditate daily and love it."

—Katherine, mama of one

Put On Your Not-Thinking Cap

While a big part of meditation is clearing the mind and not allowing random, willy-nilly thoughts to take root, I don't want to set the bar too high here just yet. As anyone who has ever tried it can tell you, purposely not thinking is really tough. Eventually, the goal is to steer your thoughts to a specific object or concept, like a candle flame or self-love. But eventually isn't now. Until you get more adept at directing your attention to a specific focus, your goal should be just gently guiding yourself back to your breath. Believe me, for beginners, that's challenging enough. But within a short time, you should be able to add another specific element to mentally hone in on, such as imagining yourself on a moonlit beach with the tide slowly lapping in and out.

I highly recommend listening to guided meditation CDs, at least in the beginning phase of your meditation practice. These provide a soft nudge to get you back on track when your mind wanders to mundane stuff, like whether you need to pick up a loaf of seven-grain bread on the way home from the office. Bernhardt's CDs are some of my favorites, as are those of Dr. Andrew Weil, which I describe in "Worked for Me." Someday I may "rough" it alone, but for now, I prefer to have a teacher along for the ride.

It's About the Journey

Whatever progress you make in incorporating yoga and meditation into your seemingly endless new-mama days and nights, be sure to appreciate yourself for your efforts. In particular, meditation requires a fair amount of stick-to-it-iveness, so go easy on yourself when you have a hard time settling down to the task at hand. And remember, "Meditation requires discipline," says Bernhardt. "So even if the whole time you were sitting there cranky and feeling like you've been having a war with your thoughts, you should pat yourself on the back."

Although yoga might take a bit of a time investment, you'll be happy to know that you can reap the benefits of meditation in a matter of minutes. But here's the catch: Those five minutes need to happen every day. After all, "The more frequently you meditate, the better you get at it—and the more you get out of it," says Alexander Kulick, MD, an integrative physician who considers meditation both a powerful stress reliever and immune booster. "Most people think they need to sit down for an hour," says Dr. Kulick, "and they know they're going to get bored. But really, meditation is just about closing your eyes for five or ten minutes. That's it. If you do it daily, you'll get as strong an impact as if you did it for a couple of hours a few times a week."

Remember, just like all your other wellness journeys—eating better, exercising more, sleeping more soundly (which we'll discuss in the next chapter)—there's no one-size-fits-all approach to yoga and meditation. So take things at your own pace and enjoy the ride. *Namasté.*

Andrew Weil CDs

With his snowy-white beard, low-key manner, and impeccable credentials (i.e., undergrad and medical degrees from Harvard), integrative health guru Andrew Weil caught my ear a long time ago. I read his books, subscribe to his online newsletter, and I'm even considering buying his Teflon-free pots and pans. In a world of "thought leaders," I just happen to trust this guy's thoughts.

So it was with nary an ounce of skepticism that I cracked open *Meditation for Optimum Health*, a two-disc CD by Dr. Weil and his colleague Jon Kabat-Zinn, PhD, an expert on mindfulness and meditation.

The first disc in the set, which I've listened to umpteen times, is kind of genius in explaining the history, inner workings, and benefits of meditation. Peppered with Thoreau and Joyce references alongside medical terms like "parasympathetic nervous system," it's at once literate and doctoresque. But a key point I seized on is the vast connection between the body and the mind. Our minds have a profound impact on our bodies and vice versa. There's truly no way to have one type of health without the other.

When I just want to dive into a short, guided meditation, I pop Dr. Weil's *Eight Meditations for Optimum Health* into my CD player. While I love all of the meditations, I'm particularly smitten with "On Loving Kindness," a core tenet of Buddhism. Throughout, Dr. Weil instructs us to channel happiness, peace, and liberation toward every living creature in the universe—including ourselves. Divine.

dream job: getting the sleep you need (and then some)

It's been estimated that new moms lose at least 700 hours of sleep the first year after their bambini arrive on the scene. Initially, that number can sound stratospheric, especially to a bleary-eyed mama bear who's too zonked out to do simple math, but basically, it shakes out to a mere 1.9 hours of lost sleep per night. For most of us, that measly number doesn't even begin to scratch the surface of our sleep deficit.

Though I had a live-in baby nurse for several months, eventually Hubby and I did have to tough it out on our own. Besides, until I started taking medication for my thyroid condition, as well as the brain-enhancement nutritional supplements I told you about in Chapter 15, my postpartum anxiety and low-grade depression generated plenty of insomnia. Trust me, I know what it's like to shuffle through my days like a zombie.

So try not to hate on me for the baby-nurse thing, and listen, with a full and open new-mommy heart, to what I'm about to share on this incredibly vital topic.

seriously, snoozing is critical

I'll go right out on a limb here and say that I believe getting enough deep sleep is the single most important thing you can do for your physical, mental, and emotional health. I even rank it above regular exercise, and we all know how vital I think that is.

Don't agree? Think you're doing just fine on five hours a night? Maybe you are—in the short term. But if you've merely accepted the fact that sleeping less is your "new postbaby normal," I'd like to steer you off that course, pronto. Because over time, it just isn't smart to skimp on shuteye. In fact, here's a short list of not-great stuff that could be headed your way if you continually shortchange yourself on sleep:

- Accelerated aging
- Anxiety and depression
- Screwed-up levels of melatonin, a megahormone that regulates your "circadian clock" (i.e., your sleep and wake cycles) and impacts menstruation, blood pressure, and your response to stress
- Lowered immunity and resistance to all sorts of illnesses, ranging from a minor cold to viral infections, heart disease, and even some forms of cancer

None of the above is meant to scare you. (Well, maybe a little. . . .) And it certainly isn't intended to piss you off, either. I know you have a cooing, drooling reason for not clocking enough time in the sack. Rather, my goal is to get you to move sleep way up on your personal priority list, even if that means other activities have to be sacrificed along the way. Or not; with some smart shuffling, you'll probably be able to at least dabble in many of your favorite prebaby hobbies. More on that in a bit.

The main job of sleep is to repair us, but unfortunately, not all sleep is created equal. Sleep occurs in stages and, though each stage is beneficial, there are two that are really crucial—REM and Stage Four NREM (aka Non-REM). I'm sure you've heard of REM sleep, but do you really know what that means? No? Well, neither did I until I started researching. Sure, I could tell you that REM was an acronym for Rapid Eye Movement, but other than that, I couldn't shed much light on the subject. But I've been doing my homework, and I'd like to gift you with this mini tutorial on the difference between the two broad categories of sleep:

NREM sleep: Roughly 80 percent of our "between-the-sheets time" is spent in NREM sleep. And it's during NREM sleep that the bulk of the restoration you're always hearing about actually occurs. This category of sleep is further divided into four different levels and Stage Four—deep sleep—is the biggie. Your body uses this chunk of time to do all of its most important work, namely repairing damaged tissue, building bone and muscle, and strengthening your immune system. If we could just snap our fingers and drop into Stage Four NREM sleep, we'd be as physically healthy as an ox.

REM sleep: This is the dream state. It's also the period in which you mentally process everything that happened during the day. Your moods are closely tied to the amount of REM you're getting—the more REM sleep you get, the cheerier you are, and vice versa. No REM = bitch on wheels. You slip into a REM pocket every ninety minutes or so, after you've cycled through the entire NREM phase. Throughout REM, your body will be as limp as an overcooked noodle. If it weren't, you'd be trying to act out your dreams, and there's nothing restful about that. Sexy maybe, if your dreams tend to get steamy, but not restful.

So now that you know a little about the basic "architecture" of sleep, let's talk about how to clear the decks for it and maximize its myriad benefits.

drop everything and haul your booty to bed

When I was pregnant and working at *Cookie* magazine, my editor in chief (the fab Pilar Guzman, a mama of two) would occasionally give me a heads up about what my new postbaby life might look like. "You'll edit your life like crazy," she'd say. "You'll see."

Upon hearing this, my first thought was, "Ouch." That just sounded so ruthless, so surgical. Who within my social circle, I wondered, would make the après-DD cut? Which of my many beloved mindless activities might get the old heave-ho? Of course, three years into this whole mom thing, I totally get it. I get it and I edit. I stay in frequent contact with close friends and family members, but I keep the surface schmoozing to a bare minimum. I figure if I'm taking time away from my tot, it has to be worth it. Ditto for my obsessions, hobbies, and mommy time-outs; now, I cherry pick. But I still manage to pack a little useless fluff into every day. I'd lose my mind if I didn't.

What does this have to do with sleep, you ask? Plenty. Here's why: I've structured my "new" life so sleep is a priority. I focus only on the essentials—i.e., mothering, working, keeping the house in some semblance of order—while everything else gets rotated and shuffled so I can get to bed by 10:00 P.M. every night.

Personally, I can't relate to staying up super late to surf the Internet or watch TV, especially considering the modern-day wonders of Tivo. And I can't even fathom skimping on sleep to do something semiworthwhile, like a load of laundry. But then again, I'm a morning person. I'd rather go to bed early and rise at the crack of dawn to do chores. And after a cup of java (or three), I can get more done in a single hour in the morning than in several at night.

Twins mama Patricia, however, is the polar opposite. After dragging through the day bone tired, she starts perking up after dinner and by 10:00 P.M. she's on fire. Still, she admits her bedtime habits are less than optimal. "Sleep experts have told me that I'm doing all the wrong things, so I take comfort in knowing I should be approaching this sleep thing differently," she says. "I'm tired all day, so at 3:00 P.M. or so I drink more coffee. At 8:00 P.M., I get a surge of energy. I get the kids to bed by 9:30 P.M., and when I finally sit down to watch *CSI* with my husband, I'm wide awake. I start writing in my blog, organizing my purse for the next day, etc., and pretty soon I hear the *Seinfeld* theme song. 'How is it 11:00?' I ask myself. We get upstairs, I wash my face, brush my teeth, and climb in bed with a book." And when, exactly, does she drift off? "I finally shut down at midnight," she says. "And when the alarm rings at 7:00 A.M., I want to shoot myself."

Just because I'm not one of them doesn't mean I can't sympathize with mamas who are natural night owls. Think how hard it must be to adjust their body clocks the second a kidlet enters the picture. After all, they've had years of going to bed anytime they damn well pleased. Take my friend Ninka, for instance. When she and I were childless singles, she always joked that she knew never to call me past 10:00 P.M. because I'd be fast asleep in my cozy bachelorette pad across town. She, meanwhile, thought nothing of staying up until 2:00 A.M. reading (stacks and stacks of British

Vogue), even when she had work the next day. Now, with two kids to tend to, she's had to do a little wheeling and dealing with her better half in order to stay up as long as she likes. "I'm very lucky," she says. "My husband takes care of the kids in the morning so I can sleep."

For those of you who don't have such understanding hubbies, or who just know you'd function better with more sleep, here's a trick I've learned for managing my prebed time: bundling. Rather than doing a little of each typical, after-the-kid-is-tucked-in activity every night (e.g., returning e-mails, chatting on the telephone, shopping online), I "bundle" them and monotask. One night, I whip through my computer inbox. Another night is set aside for plowing through catalogs, snail, and junk mail. On another night, I'll call a friend or family member. My point is, I don't even attempt to do all that stuff in a single evening. And if you're chronically sleep deprived, perhaps you shouldn't, either.

turning off and tuning out: practicing "good sleep hygiene"

It's a weird phrase, but the basic habits of setting the stage for slumber are known together as "good sleep hygiene." Here's the Dana version of all the steps you should take (and stuff you should avoid) if you want to sleep like, well, a baby:

- **Put a cork in it:** You've heard it before, but it bears repeating: As good as booze is at knocking you out, it messes with your REM sleep. So consider steering clear, at least on school nights. And lay off the coffee after 4:00 P.M., too. That will give the caffeine time to wear off.
- **Back away from the fridge:** No big meals right before bed, although a light snack is fine. You don't want your stomach going into digestion overdrive when you're trying to doze off.

- **Finish working out at least four hours before bed:** Otherwise, there's a chance you'll get all hopped up and energized, and that's no state of mind/body in which to sail off to Sleepy Town. Yoga might be okay, but why risk it?

- **Spring for comfy bedding:** You don't need to spend a fortune (unless you want to), but at least splash out on high-quality sheets and a great pillow.

- **Develop routines:** Go to bed at the same time, wake up at the same time, do the same "wind-down" things in the same way, religiously. (See my night-night routine in "Worked for Me.") Practicing the same routine nightly will help send sleep cues to your mind and body.

- **Keep your bedroom dark, quiet, and cold:** From the digital clock to street lamps, we underestimate all the light creeping into our bedrooms at night; I've actually taken to wearing a mask. If you sleep with a snorer, buy earplugs. And as for the chilly temperature, that's what blankets are for.

- **Reserve your bed for sleeping and sexing:** This is a toughie, because who doesn't have a flatscreen and a pile of books in their bedroom? At the very least, don't drag your laptop or anything else work related in there. You want your mind and body to associate your bedroom with sleep, not every other activity known to (wo)man.

- **Zap the nap:** A midday snooze throws off your circadian rhythm, which makes it harder to fall asleep at night. If you're completely exhausted, limit your nap to fifteen minutes. If you're zonked out long enough to get through all the NREM and REM cycles, you'll wake up anything but refreshed.

- **Get up if it just ain't happening:** After about ten sleepless minutes, cut your losses, get out of bed, and head somewhere else in the house. Then do something boring and snoozeworthy, such as watching a rerun of a show you've already seen about ninety-five times. When you find yourself dozing off, head back to Sleep Central.

Of course, the best-laid plans can easily go awry, especially for those with wee ones in the house. And any mother with a newborn and other small fries is doubly challenged in the sleep department. "My youngest has only been sleeping through the night for eight months," says Jeanine, mama of two. "So the first months after he arrived were definitely a killer. I found myself depressed during that time, which I attributed to lack of sleep. I still have nights when my oldest is up during the night, but I usher him right back to bed. And I stay firm about him sleeping in his own bed." Sounds like a smart strategy to me.

reserve the right to . . .

. . . ask everyone in your household to pitch in when you're going through a rough patch sleepwise. Knowing you don't have a pile of dirty dishes or a mountain of laundry to get through before you hit the hay can make a huge difference in helping you clear your mind, which is the first step in drifting off.

when mr. sandman goes missing

For most of you, "insomnia" is probably a foreign word. It's all you can do to keep your peepers propped open, right? But for anyone suffering from postpartum anxiety or depression, restful sleep can go utterly AWOL. Maybe you lie awake for hours before finally nodding off or, as with me, staying asleep is the problem. Even if you nod off fairly quickly, twiddling your thumbs in the middle of the night will ultimately result in a lousy night's sleep, too.

Here's a typical new-mama Catch-22: You're feeling low and stressed to the max from caring for your tot all day, so you have trouble falling or staying asleep. Because of all that tossing and turning, you never get through enough of the total sleep cycle to reach REM, which is essentially the stress-relieving stage, the stretch of time in which we process and consolidate emotions. Not to mention the fact that REM sleep is also key to learning and developing new skills, like, say, mothering a newborn for the first time. It's a vicious circle.

Something else to consider: Because deep sleep—Stage Four NREM—ranks so high in the human-body pecking order, when we're sleep deprived, our bodies naturally make up this "sleep debt" before replenishing REM. That means your emotional state can take a backseat to your physical health until your sleep debt is repaid. Personally, I'd take the sniffles over a case of the blues any day.

While the good sleep habits outlined above may help, insomnia can be persistent and powerful. Nine times out of ten, it takes root because we're ruminating over how the day played out. But try not to just lie there stewing over some trivial matter (or even a big one); make peace with the twenty-four-hour stretch that just flashed by and be done with it.

the**mother**load

"Let's face it, no woman has ever really, truly slept her deepest sleep after becoming a mother—we just aren't programmed that way. But feeling your kids are safe is an important start. And I have a few other tricks I try to use on a regular basis (other than Ambien, which, from time to time, certainly helps): I take a bath or at least put my feet in a warm bucket of water for fifteen minutes, and I drink warm water with lemon or another hot beverage like green tea. Also, when I try to get into bed at the same time for a week, that somehow gets my system back on track."

—Jill E., mama of two

By the way, harnessing your self-talk and keeping a journal (remember Chapters 13 and 14?) are massively helpful in releasing negativity and steering your thoughts in a happy, more sleep-friendly direction. If you've slacked off on either of those, you might want to revisit.

One last point: If sleeplessness doesn't let up, see your physician to determine if there are any underlying medical problems keeping you awake at night. Sleep is crazy-important. Make it, yourself, and your no-stones-unturned Momover a priority.

A Nightly Ritual

Apart from nights when I wake up at 3:00 A.M. and can't doze back off for love or money, I sleep well. And while I know that that's largely due to my thyroid meds and nutritional supplements, I'm also convinced that my prebed routine is a big help.

Since it's lights out at 10:00 P.M. for me, I start the wheels in motion no later than 9:30. After slipping into my nightie, I remove all jewelry except my beloved Q-Link necklace (*www.q-linkproducts.com*), which is imbedded with a tiny chip that allegedly reduces stress by shielding wearers from the damage from all the electromagnetic waves hurling at us from our cell phones, computers, GPS devices, etc. Maybe it's all a load of rubbish. All I know is that I sleep well when I wear my Q-Link, and not so hot when I don't.

Next, I give my face a thorough scrubbing, because as any dermatologist worth his Botox needle will tell you, removing makeup and the day's grime is much more important than washing your face when you wake up. (In fact, if you're pressed for time and washed your face thoroughly before bed, you can simply splash water on it in the morning.)

Depending on whether I think my complexion needs to "breathe," I may or may not slather on an overnight miracle cream. Next I brush and floss, followed by my all-important, head-to-toe dry brushing that I told you about in Chapter 16. If I'm bushed, I dry brush before everything else. It gives me that slight zap of energy I need to get through the washing, flossing, and whatnot.

Finally, I do something just for me: I dab patchouli on my wrists and neck. Because it's so hippie-granola and polarizing—meaning people either love it or hate it—I don't wear patchouli during the day. In fact, my super-crisp, ocean-themed "signature scent" is pretty much the exact opposite. But I happen to love patchouli; it makes me happy. And being happy before you drift off to sleep is a very good thing indeed.

staying on the front burner

This is the grand finale, my last opportunity to convince you of the importance of making yourself priority *numero uno*, of doing everything in your power and using all the tools at your disposal to optimize your mental, physical, and spiritual health. So please forgive the sense of urgency in my tone here. I'm just laying it all on the line so you'll keep your Momover going full tilt—just like I'll be doing.

Listen, on the self-care front, no one can be a bigger slug than me. A few months ago, I didn't work out for two solid weeks because of a stomach virus that lasted, oh, maybe forty-eight hours. And my self-talk is a major work in progress. When I start "living inside my head," as I call it, it can take a huge effort to pull myself back out.

But here's what I've noticed: When I'm in a good groove of exercising and eating well, meditating and minding my stress levels, I gain momentum. For instance, if I work out twice one week, I'll shoot for three times the following week and four times the week after that. And I'll keep up with all my little "health hits," like squeezing lemon into my water to balance my pH level or eating spinach for lunch rather than just inhaling a gigantic block of chocolate. Of course I've done chocolate block bit, but then I usually overcompensate by not eating anything for the rest of the day, including dinner. So it's not quite worth it, is it? Then there's the spiritual stuff I'll tackle, like stealing a few minutes every day to meditate or reread *The Four Agreements* for the thousandth time.

I've seen this good-momentum thing described as a "virtuous circle," and I like the idea of that. Basically it just boils down to the better you do, the better you want to do. It's certainly preferable to the dreaded opposite thought process, which says, "I haven't worked out in a week; why bother hauling my ass to the gym today?"

Clearly, a Momover is an ongoing journey, with lots of twists and turns along the way. Yes, it's work, but so is caring for a newborn, not to mention raising that delicious DD into a strong, happy, well-rounded miss or mister. So it's not as if you're not already in "work mode." Besides, putting yourself on the top of your to-do list yields two gigantic benefits. One, you'll have that much more stamina and get up and go to take care of your tot. Two, you'll feel confident, resilient, and strong the entire time you're doing it. What mama bear could possibly say no to that plan?

check in with yourself

So let's say that as you've been reading this book, you've been tin-kering and fussing, trying a little something new here and there. Or maybe you've even had a few weeks in which you were an abso-lute rock star—hitting the home gym regularly, eating your organic blueberries and Brussels sprouts, skipping the late-night infomer-cial surfing in favor of a few more hours of sleep. Brava! Now comes the hard part: Keeping it up.

Motivation is personal. You're the only one who can nudge your-self in the right self-care direction. Sure, you have a powerful incen-tive sitting in that high chair over there, covered in mashed carrots and flashing one of those impossibly adorable gummy smiles. But as center of the universe as he may be, your baby can't make you hop on that treadmill or swallow that teaspoon of flaxseed oil. Only you can do that.

So what's the best way to find out what you need? Stay on top of what's going on. By keeping a journal, or even some version of my self-care chart, you can easily detect when you've slacked off in certain areas, be it eating well or remembering to do your deep breathing when you're feeling freaked. Another way to assess your state of mind and body is to set aside an hour or two once a month for a deeper analysis. (Totally doable, by the way; just mark it on your calendar, all official like.)

Keep in mind that taking on big "extra-credit" assignments, whether it's throwing a birthday bash or offering to coach the Sat-urday morning soccer team, obviously means more stress. Even if you handle a heavier workload in a healthy way—by staying upbeat and focused and chipping away at it in small chunks every day—you're still absorbing additional mental strain, whether you're aware of it or not. By checking in with yourself, you'll be able to recognize when you need to up the ante on the relaxation front. Maybe that means committing to yoga class on a more regu-lar basis or carving out the time for a standing Saturday afternoon nap. (Just remember Chapter 18, and keep it brief!) Whatever you do, just make sure it supports the ultimate goal of your Momover, which is head-to-toe health.

reserve the right to . . .

. . . cue the music. This just in: Right as I was putting the finishing touches on this book, new research emerged that supported something I'd long suspected—that listening to music we really love makes us not only happy, but healthy, too. How? By lowering our blood pressure and heart rates and boosting our self-healing hormones. So dig out your favorite CDs and keep 'em in heavy rotation. Whether it's old-school heavy metal or a Disney Princesses movie soundtrack you "borrowed" from your DD, you'll get an instant hit of health and happiness.

To find the weak links in your own personal health chain, you have to pose the questions in order to get the answers. So ask yourself, "What do I need? What have I been neglecting lately that could really help re-energize me? How can I recharge my batteries?" Just think of this self-analysis as a trip to the doctor that doesn't require hopping in the car or writing a check at the end. In other words, take a cue from your own medical experts and poke around a bit.

adjust and tweak your health regimens

Most of what I was referring to above is lifestyle related—beefing up your fitness, nutrition, sleep, and relaxation routines when you feel you need a little extra oomph. But there are bound to be times when you need to seek the counsel of trained professionals, when whatever you're experiencing can't be solved with more leafy greens or an extra hour of shuteye. And you should always check with your physician before switching up anything for which you're already under medical supervision. And definitely don't go hopping off any prescription meds just because you're feeling better or because the condition you're being treated for seems to have been alleviated. It's also a good idea to speak to your doctor before embracing any substantial health shifts like, say, embarking on a major fitness plan or becoming a vegetarian.

To be at your best, I think it's really important to realize that your health status is ever changing. How you felt six months ago—heck, even six days ago—may have little bearing on how you're feeling right now. And it's not all physiological; what's going on in your life has a huge impact on your health. Maybe your baby is teething and keeping the whole house awake at night. Or perhaps you've just changed jobs. In our warp-speed, twenty-first-century lives, status quo doesn't really exist anymore. As a new mom, change is the one constant in your life.

If you've been keeping up with all your crucial screening exams (and hopefully sprinkling in some "extra-credit" tests as well), adjustments and tweaks to your health regimen might be dictated by those results. Maybe you'll add iron or vitamin D to your supplement arsenal or be advised to make a more concerted effort to eat low-fat foods. Still others (like me) might be advised to never leave the house without applying sunscreen first.

themotherload

"Motherhood has forced me to be more focused, which has had a positive effect on my whole life. When I'm at the office, I'm motivated to get things done so that I can get home as soon as possible to be with my daughter. No more procrastinating, no more idle hours spent surfing the Internet, no more stewing over slights—perceived or real. I also find that I'm that able to leave work completely behind when I get home and focus on being in the moment. Save for those moments when she's having a tantrum, I find my time with my child electrifying."

—**Jenny B.**, mama of one

At other times, changes will be driven simply by instinct and the way you feel. You'll know when your energy is flagging, when you're feeling more anxious than usual, or when your stomach is out of sorts. So listen to yourself and experiment, and keep a record of the changes you're making and how your body, mind, and spirit are reacting. That's really the most efficient way to raise your health game.

Because we mama bears are so accustomed to caring for everyone else but ourselves, paying all that attention to yourself might feel funny at first. Do it anyway; eventually it will become second nature.

seek out feel-good gurus

It's no secret that I'm passionate about mama health—my own and everyone else's. Maybe if I were ten years younger than I was when I had my DD, or if I hadn't had such a rocky postpartum recovery, I might not be as obsessive-compulsive about the whole postbaby wellness thing. But guess what? I am. And I don't think this leopard will be changing her spots anytime soon. Still, I'm not so fixated that I run around to doctors and wellness experts all day long. The only ones I see on a regular basis are my primary care physician, my dermatologist, my gynecologist, and my dentist. Oh, and I chat with a life coach on occasion. But that's it. Believe me, some of my mom friends have way more experts on speed dial, from acupuncturists and internists to plastic surgeons and podiatrists.

Of course, I'm lucky, because my job as a health and beauty journalist has put me in contact with a lot of superstar docs and gurus over the years. Beyond just talking with me for magazine articles, some have even made specific personal recommendations based on medical tests they've conducted.

I realize that not everyone lives in the New York area or happens to work in a profession that throws them in the path of renowned health professionals, but that doesn't mean you can't tap their knowledge. Whether I've specifically interviewed them or simply recommended their work in the Dig Deeper Appendix, I've peppered this book with experts from whom I think you could learn a great deal. I encourage you to explore what they have to say and incorporate whatever you feel works for your life—and your physical, emotional, and spiritual health!

And by all means, assemble your own team of go-to gurus. Maybe there's an amazing massage therapist at your local day spa, someone who routinely leaves you feeling totally blissed out and centered. Or perhaps your friend recommended a kick-ass personal trainer or a dietician who's a whiz at figuring out exactly what vitamins and minerals you need. And don't discount your regular beauty-maintenance squad. I love popping into my colorist's salon for a few hours every four weeks. I drink a glass of wine, catch up on a little harmless celebrity gossip, and get my roots zapped at the same time. Without question, Anthony, who has "blonded" me for eons, is one of my most trusted feel-good/look-good gurus. Be sure to surround yourself with your own.

the momover mantras

Okay, technically we're at the end of our Momover journey—at least the one we've been taking together in the pages of this book. But the one you're taking on your own? Hopefully, that won't end anytime soon.

To make the road easier, I've whipped up this handy list of Momover Mantras. On some days, the physical-health mantra might strike a chord. On other days, you could be in need of a spiritual lift. But this list of simple mantras represents everything I'm hoping for you, now and forever:

- I value my mental health, and I make sure to surround myself with friends, family, and the support networks I need.

- I value my physical health, and I make sure to exercise, eat well, and keep up with all of my necessary medical screenings.
- I value my emotional and spiritual health, and I make sure to relax, take lots of mommy mini breaks, and speak to myself in a loving manner.

I recommend jotting the mantras down on index cards and stashing them in places they might come in handy, such as your purse, desk drawer at work, and nightstand. Just think of them as the mommy version of your tot's flash cards and whip 'em out any time you need a little extra oomph!

Remember, keeping up with your Momover isn't (intrinsically) about how you look, but rather about how you feel. Just focus and put your best (pedicured or otherwise) foot forward. And it would be good if you stayed mid-Momover for basically the next twenty years. Re-evaluating your health status—inside and outside, top to bottom—on a regular basis is the best way to stay on top of your game, for yourself and your child. Think about it: What better way to ensure a bright future for your family than by keeping yourself in tip-top shape?

There isn't a doubt in my mind that you can do it. So be well, mama.

dig deeper appendix: helpful books, websites, and dvds

This resource guide, which is organized by book chapter, is jam packed with all of the tools I've found helpful in my new-mom life. Because I know how limited your time is, particularly with the website recommendations, I've drilled down to what I consider the most mama-essential info. And as always, I encourage you to keep learning—about yourself and your new baby.

chapter one: handling home-from-the-hospital freakouts

Puryear, Lucy J. *Understanding Your Moods When You're Expecting: Emotions, Mental Health, and Happiness—Before, During, and After Pregnancy.* (New York: Houghton Mifflin Company, 2007).

www.AskDrSears.com
Website of famous pediatrician William Sears. Must click: "The Postpartum Period."

www.dona.org
Website of DONA International (Doulas of North America International). Must click: "Postpartum Doula FAQs." Also provides a directory for finding a postpartum doula in your area.

www.familyeducation.com
Must clicks: "Postpartum Recovery," a guide that stretches from the first week to a full year after baby, and "New Mom Survival Strategies," a sizeable archive of articles on a range of topics.

chapter two: call in the troops

www.babysittersacrossamerica.com
A coast-to-coast enterprise offering the services of prescreened sitters.

www.citymommy.com
Originally launched in L.A., this membership-only, local community website is up to twenty-five chapters (and counting) across the country.

🖱 *www.sensiblesitters.com*
If you're lucky enough to live in N.Y., L.A., the Hamptons, or the Palm Beach area, this is a treasure trove of highly screened babysitters and full-time nannies.

🖱 *www.whattoexpect.com*
Website of the "What To Expect When You're Expecting" books. Must click: Message boards in the "Community" section, which feature all types of moms (i.e., multiples and twins, military, food allergies, etc.).

🖱 *www.workitmom.com*
Bills itself as "Blogs, resources and community for working moms." Must click: "Balancing Act"—articles by members.

chapter three: baby step into your brand-new life

Moran, Victoria. *Creating A Charmed Life: Sensible, Spiritual Secrets Every Busy Woman Should Know.* (San Francisco: HarperSanFrancisco, 1999).

Niven, David. *The 100 Simple Secrets of Happy Families: What Scientists Have Learned and How You Can Use It.* (San Francisco: HarperSanFrancisco, 2004).

Simpson, Bria. *The Balanced Mom: Raising Your Kids Without Losing Your Self.* (Oakland, CA: New Harbinger Publications, 2006).

🖱 *www.motherhoodtransitions.com*
Website of life coach Gretchen Reid. Must click: "Additional Resources," a collection of articles by Reid on the topics of balance, work, and motherhood and what she calls "motherhood development."

chapter four: checkups: one for baby, one for you

🖱 *www.labtestsonline.org*
Bills itself as "a public resource on clinical lab testing from the laboratory professionals who do the testing"; offers a searchable database of screening tests as well as conditions—e.g., under "anemia," a common postpartum health issue, you'll learn about causes, associated screening tests, and related website links.

🖱 *www.themorrisoncenter.com*
The official website of Jeffrey Morrison, MD, and his New York City integrative medical practice. Must click: "Conditions We Treat," which includes several informative, not-too-techy medical-journal articles and papers he's written on such topics as heavy-metal toxicity and the effects of stress.

Roizen, Michael F., and Mehmet C. Oz. *You: The Owner's Manual—An Insider's Guide to the Body That Will Make You Healthier and Younger.* (New York: HarperResource, 2005).

🖱 *www.womenshealth.gov*
Maintained by the U.S. Department of Health & Human Services; bills itself as "the federal government source for women's health information"; great source for free printable pamphlets and downloadable PDF files. Must clicks: "Common Screening And Diagnostic Tests" and "Screening Tests And Immunization Guidelines for Women."

chapter five: the six-month window (tapping ma nature's get-back-in-shape help)

Chabut, La Reine. *Lose That Baby Fat: Bouncing Back the First Year After Having a Baby.* (New York: Evans, 2006).

Denney, Stacy, and Kate Hodson. *Fit Mama: A Real-Life Fitness Guide for the New Mom.* (San Francisco: Chronicle Books, 2007).

Kirsch, David. *Sound Mind, Sound Body: David Kirsch's Ultimate 6-Week Transformation for Men and Women.* (New York: Rodale, 2002).

⌐ᐤ *www.mommywithoutpounds.com*
Although the printable "Complete Mommy Kit" (exercise manual and journal, goal tracker and weight-loss chart, recipes for busy moms) isn't free, viewing the highly motivating before-and-after photos is.

chapter six: restoke your engine

⌐ᐤ *www.endfatigue.com*
Website of Dr. Jacob Teitelbaum, an expert in the areas of sleep, energy, fatigue, and pain. Must click: "General Health Issues," which contains several key sections, including "Nutrition Overview" and "Vitality Pyramid."

Freston, Kathy. *Quantum Wellness: A Practical and Spiritual Guide to Heath and Happiness.* (New York: Weinstein Books, 2008)

Gordon, Jon. *Energy Addict: 101 Physical, Mental, and Spiritual Ways to Energize Your Life.* (New York: Perigee, 2003).

Raffelock, Dean, and Robert Rountree. *A Natural Guide to Pregnancy and Postpartum Health.* (New York: Avery, 2002).

Roizen, Michael F., and Mehmet C. Oz. *You: Being Beautiful: The Owner's Manual to Inner and Outer Beauty.* (New York: Free Press, 2008).

chapter seven: step away from the cupcake: "eating for two" is officially over

Freedman, Rory, and Kim Barnouin. *Skinny Bitch Bun in the Oven: A Gutsy Guide to Becoming One Hot and Healthy Mother.* (Philadelphia: Running Press, 2008).

Keller, Jackie. *Body After Baby: A Simple, Healthy Plan to Lose Your Body Weight Fast.* (New York: Penguin Group, 2006).

www.lifescript.com
A women's health website that counts *Women's Bodies, Women's Wisdom* author Dr. Christiane Northrup as one of its resident experts. Must click: "Weight Loss Basics."

Somer, Elizabeth. *10 Habits That Mess Up a Woman's Diet: Simple Strategies to Eat Right, Lose Weight and Reclaim Your Health.* (New York: McGraw-Hill, 2006).

Zinczenko, David, with Matt Goulding. *Eat This, Not That! Supermarket Survival Guide: The No-Diet Weight Loss Solution.* (New York: Rodale, 2009).

www.womentowomen.com
Website of the famous Women to Women clinic in Maine, a pioneer in female-only care. Must click: "Diet, Nutrition & Weight Loss," which features several excellent articles on eating for optimal health and curbing postpartum food cravings.

chapter eight: exercise: to baby or not to baby

Druxman, Lisa, with Martica Heaner. *Lean Mommy: Bond With Your Baby and Get Fit With the StrollerStrides Program.* (New York: Hachette Book Group, 2007).

www.mommyandmeworkout.com
Source of DVDs modeled after the popular Pasadena-based Mommy & Me Workout classes. Targeted to specific ages from three months to five years, the DVDs are available in yoga-dance, tap and acrobatics, and ballet and stretch formats.

DVD: *The Perfect Postnatal Workout.* Ideal for exercising with a young (read: fairly lightweight and easily hoistable) baby. Available at Amazon.

Staton, Laura, and Sarah Perron. *Baby Om: Yoga for Mothers and Babies.* (New York: Henry Holt and Company, 2002).

chapter nine: the fast and the furious

Johnson-Cane, Diedre, Jonathan Cane, and Joe Glickman. *The Complete Idiot's Guide to Short Workouts.* (Indianapolis: Alpha Books, 2001).

DVD: *Joyce Vedral: Complete Definition Workout Series Plus Bonus Abs.* Available at Amazon. (Note: Vedral sells several body part-specific DVDs at her own website, *www.joycevedral.com*; this one works the entire body in short time blocks, but broken up by different zones on different days.)

DVD: *Ten Minute Solution: Target Toning for Beginners.* Features five separate ten-minute segments for arms, shoulders, abs, butt, thighs, plus "power stretching." Available at Amazon.

Ungaro, Alycea. *15 Minute Everyday Pilates.* (New York: DK Publishing, 2008).

chapter ten: ab solution

Chabut, La Reine. *Core Strength for Dummies.* (Hoboken, New Jersey: Wiley Publishing Inc., 2008).

DVD: *Lindsay Brin's Core Fitness for Moms.* Emphasizes pelvic floor and transverse abdominus muscle, bypassing traditional crunches. Includes beginner, intermediate, and advanced routines as well as tips on nutrition and weight loss. Available at Amazon.

www.surgery.org
Website of The American Society of Aesthetic Plastic Surgery. Must clicks: "Patient Safety Tips" and the "Ask the Right Questions" in the Consumer Information section.

Tupler, Julie, with Jodie Gould. *Lose Your Mummy Tummy.* (New York: Da Capo, 2005).

chapter eleven: breast intentions

www.breastimplantsafety.org
Joint website venture between the American Society for Aesthetic Plastic Surgery and the American Society of Plastic Surgeons. Offers a wealth of info covering virtually every aspect of augmentation. Must click: "Safety, Risks and Benefits."

🖱 *www.center4research.com*

Website of the National Research Center for Women & Families. Must click: The "Women's Health" section, which features numerous articles on breast-implant safety as well as information regarding the impact of breast surgery on breastfeeding.

🖱 *www.expertvillage.com*

Must see: A series of short, instructional bra-related videos, including "Proper Bra Fit" and "Bra Sizes From Different Manufacturers" located in the "Fashion, Style and Personal Care" section of the site.

🖱 *www.lindasonline.com*

Website of expert bra fitter Linda Becker. Must click: "Bra School," which includes info on fit, style, problems, and proper care. You can also purchase several different brands here.

chapter twelve: the power of primping

Brandt, Fredric. *10 Minutes, 10 Years: Your Definitive Guide to a Beautiful and Youthful Appearance.* (New York: Free Press, 2007).

Farr, Kendall. *The Pocket Stylist: Behind-the-Scenes Expertise from a Fashion Pro on Creating Your Own Unique Look.* (New York: Gotham Books, 2004).

France, Kim, and Andrea Linett. *The Lucky Shopping Manual: Building and Improving Your Wardrobe Piece by Piece.* (New York: Gotham Books, 2003).

Kashuk, Sonia. *Real Beauty.* (New York: Clarkson Potter, 2003).

Woodall, Trinny, and Susannah Constantine. *What You Wear Can Change Your Life.* (New York: Riverhead Books, 2004).

chapter thirteen: watch your mouth: the importance of positive self-talk

Helmstetter, Shad. *What to Say When You Talk to Yourself.* (New York: Pocket Books, 1982).

www.pickthebrain.com
This self-improvement website is packed with material geared toward five broad categories, including motivation, personal productivity, and philosophy. Must click: "7 Steps to Positive Self Talk."

www.selftalk.org
Website of self-talk pioneer Shad Helmstetter. If you read one of his books (i.e., the one listed above) and want to learn more, this is a comprehensive source of CDs directed at specific issues, including weight loss and self-esteem for kids.

Seligman, Martin. *Learned Optimism: How To Change Your Mind and Your Life.* (New York: Pocket Books, 1990).

chapter fourteen: the write stuff

www.journalingforhappiness.com
Website of Toronto-based journaling guru Maureen Daigle-Weaver. I've found her "Conscious Living E-Zine," which you have to subscribe to, full of solid tips on journaling and other self-improvement topics.

Klauser, Henriette Anne. *Write It Down, Make It Happen: Knowing What You Want—And Getting It!* (New York: Fireside, 2000).

🖱 *www.themomblogs.com*
This website features a massive collection of blogs written by mothers as well as tips and encouragement for starting one of your own.

Morris, Janet Terban. *The Simplify Journal: A Workbook to Help You Regain Control of Your Life.* (White Plains, NY: Peter Pauper Press, 2002).

chapter fifteen: stress is worse than a dirty diapee

🖱 *www.americanheart.org*
Website of the American Heart Association. As the number-one killer of American women, heart disease is a subject every mama should learn more about. There's so much here, including a great "Heart Health Toolbox" with lots of downloadable PDFs. Must click: "Reducing Stress" section.

Elliott, Charles H., and Laura L. Smith. *Overcoming Anxiety for Dummies.* (New York: Wiley Publishing Inc., 2002).

Kirshenbaum, Mira. *The Emotional Energy Factor: The Secrets High-Energy People Use to Beat Emotional Fatigue.* (New York: Delacorte Press, 2003).

Hodson, Kate. *The New Mom's Stress Survival Kit.* (San Francisco: Chronicle Books, 2006). This sweet little boxed set includes a sleep mask emblazoned with "New Mom: Do Not Disturb" and thirty tiny flashcards with how-to info on tension busters such as "Learn to Delegate" and "Soak Those Toes."

Somer, Elizabeth. *Food and Mood: The Complete Guide to Eating Well and Feeling Your Best, 2nd ed.* (New York: Henry Holt, 1999).

chapter sixteen: time-outs aren't just for tykes

Denney, Stacy. *Spa Mama: Pampering for the Mother-to-Be.* (San Francisco: Chronicle Books, 2005).

Stern, Lyss, and Julie Klappas. *If You Give a Mom a Martini: 100 Ways to Find 10 Blissful Minutes for Yourself.* (New York: Clarkson Potter, 2009).

chapter seventeen: the om stretch

www.gaiam.com
From ergonomic rattan chairs and singing bowls to cork blocks and hemp mats, this one-stop shopping website stocks an array of yoga and meditation tools and DVDs. Must click: "Wellness Clinic," an in-depth product section featuring a series of videos created in conjunction with the Mayo Clinic.

Haddon, Dayle. *The 5 Principles of Ageless Living: A Woman's Guide to Lifelong Health, Beauty, and Well-Being.* (New York: Atria Books, 2003).

Harp, David, and Nina Smiley. *The Three Minute Meditator: Fifth Completely Revised Edition.* (Mind's I Press, 2007). To order: *www .thethreeminutemeditator.com*

DVD: *Seane Corn, Vinyasa Flow Yoga Session One; Seane Corn Vinyasa Flow Yoga Session Two.* Both of these are filmed live and unscripted, for a realistic one-on-one, instructor-student experience and both delve into the spiritual aspects of yoga alongside proper form. Available at Gaiam.com.

chapter eighteen: dream job: getting the sleep you need (and then some)

🖱 *www.bettersleep.org*
The website of the Better Sleep Council, this elevates sound snoozing to an art form. Must Click: "The Ideal Bedroom" in the "Mattressology" section, featuring tons of tips for creating a "sleep sanctuary."

Roizen, Michael F., and Mehmet C. Oz. *You: Staying Young: The Owner's Manual for Extending Your Warranty.* (New York: Free Press, 2007).

🖱 *www.sleepfoundation.org*
The website of the National Sleep Foundation, offering much more information than the average mama probably will ever need to know about shuteye. Must click: "Sleeping Smart," located in the "Sleep Facts and Information" section, which debunks a slew of slumber myths.

Weil, Andrew. *8 Weeks to Optimum Health: A Proven Program for Taking Full Advantage of Your Body's Natural Healing Power.* (New York: Knopf, 1997).

Index

About the Author

Dana Wood began her career as a cub reporter for *Women's Wear Daily* and has been a beauty journalist for nearly twenty years. She has been the Beauty Director of *W* and the Health & Beauty Director of *Cookie*. Additionally, she has written for numerous national publications, including *Glamour*, *Harper's Bazaar*, *InStyle*, *Women's Health*, *SELF*, and *People*. She has also spent several years as an Assistant Vice President of Strategic Development for the Luxury Products Division of L'Oreal USA. In November 2007, she returned to *W* as the Senior Fashion Features Editor.

In 2006, during her stint at *Cookie*, Wood had her first child at age forty-three. Shortly thereafter, she launched "Momover," an online column on Cookiemag.com that explores the collision of age and first-time mommy-hood, or, as it was then subtitled, "the back-from-the-brink beauty journey of a really-not-young first-time mother." That column, along with lots of mama-centric wellness content—for the mind, body, and spirit and mothers of all ages—now lives at Momover.net.